Strong Women Rising

STRONG WOMEN RISING

How to Step into Your Power,
Boost Your Confidence, and
Improve Your Life

BY TIFFANY REESE

Illustrations by Jacky Sheridan

ROCKRIDGE
PRESS

For general information on our other products and services or to obtain technical support, please contact our Customer Care Department within the United States at (866) 744-2665, or outside the United States at (510) 253-0500.

Rockridge Press publishes its books in a variety of electronic and print formats. Some content that appears in print may not be available in electronic books, and vice versa.

Interior and Cover Designer: Tricia Jang
Art Producer: Megan Baggott
Editor: Morgan Shanahan
Production Editor: Mia Moran
Illustrations © 2020 Jacky Sheridan
Author photo courtesy of Danny Offer

ISBN: Print 978-1-64611-541-9 | eBook 978-1-64611-542-6

R0

Michael

Thank you for helping me become the strong woman I am today. I am forever grateful for the support you have freely given and for the sacrifices you have made to help me pursue my passions.

Jude, Ruby, AND Ozzy

You are my everything, and your love fuels me to be better each day.

Contents

As we struggle to balance work, life, bills, and relationships and meet society's (and, let's be real, our own ridiculously high) expectations, sometimes it can feel like the world is working against us. Just making it to Friday can feel like a struggle. So how can we pursue our dreams when we're stuck in a rut or feel that obstacles in our way are too high? We'll get into that. For, like, 150 pages. TL;DR: If you're looking to cockblock doubt and excuses, this is the book for you.

If you're getting anxiety sweats already, remind yourself of this: Staying where you are now is MORE PAINFUL than working toward where you want to be. Yes, it's going to be a lot of work. Yes, you're going to have to step outside your comfort zone. And, yes, you may even have to ask someone for help. Gross, I know. Yet no matter how hard your goals seem in the abstract, you got this.

First, we're going to dig into the things that weigh us down from reaching our highest potential. We all have bullshit to unpack. Carrying self-doubt, shame, and negativity gets heavy—it's time to offload these freeloading assholes and get hustling.

You are valuable, amazing, inspiring, and capable. We're going to get all up into how awesome you are (whether you like it or not). Recognizing our strengths and gifts is as important as pinpointing our challenges. Once we have shifted through our barriers and advantages, we will dig into creating goals, developing an action plan, and pursuing our passions with purpose.

Through concrete and actionable tips, we're going to stop overthinking and start kicking ass. Grab a coffee and a pencil—it's about to get productive AF.

CHAPTER 1

Reprogramming Your Thoughts *and* Deleting Negativity

(Probably Your Browser History, Too)

> "If you do not run your subconscious mind yourself,
> someone else will run it for you."
>
> —Florence Scovel Shinn, *artist and author*

Conscious (*adjective*) The stuff we're thinking about right now. The part of our brain we use in the moment—with our homies the five senses

Subconscious (*adjective*) Our brain's hard drive. The place we store all of our memories and shit

Austrian neurologist, founder of psychoanalysis, and brain dude Sigmund Freud created the psychoanalytic theory of personality. This is the idea that the conscious mind consists of everything inside our awareness while our subconscious mind (also referred to as our preconscious mind) accesses things we might not be presently aware of but that can be pulled into our conscious awareness when needed. Like when the Spice Girls' "Wannabe" comes on and you remember every damn *zigga-zig-ahh*.

I like to think of our subconscious as our brain's hard drive. This backup drive stores all our knowledge and experiences, the good, the bad, and the fugly. Freud believed that our stored memories (subconscious) influence our current (conscious) awareness. Our "programming" influences the decisions we make today. This can contaminate the amount of confidence we hold in ourselves and what we feel we can accomplish.

For example, when you were growing up, if your mom always told you that math was for boys and that you just weren't good at math (same), you may have trusted and believed this idea and avoided any activity that involved math. Until one day you realized maybe you could enjoy math, but you've simply never tried. Our subconscious can sometimes hold us back from living our #BestLife. The human mind is very impressionable, and we assume our past experiences, successes, and failures will automatically dictate the outcomes of our future endeavors.

Your subconscious also stores lots of helpful information needed to reach your goals. This is the part of your mind that you're going to leverage in pursuing your passions.

WTF Is Reality, Anyway?

Thinking something does not make it true.
Wanting something does not make it real.
—Michelle Hodkin, author

> **Reality** (*noun*) The state or quality of being real, hashtag authentic. Facts. Receipts. Real shit

Our construct of reality has been forming since the moment we slipped out of the womb. How, where, and when we were raised influences the *why* behind what we believe. Growing up, I was told that being physically attractive was basically a woman's purpose here on earth. In order to be valuable, you needed to be "hot."

I never met the standards of physical attractiveness my parents had for me and was a constant disappointment and embarrassment to them. When someone would pay me a compliment about the way I looked, my mother would tell me they were just feeling sorry for me. Kids at school weren't much better. Little assholes found me to be an easy target because I was fat. I dreaded shopping for clothes with my mom more than anything else. This embedded self-hatred in me at a very young age. The first time I thought about killing myself, I was eight years old.

As I got older, I realized what fucking jerks my parents were. A lot of their behavior was a product of their own negative programming. And I learned they had mental health issues that worsened the situation. I moved out at 17 and began to attempt to separate myself from the cesspool of emotional abuse that was my home life.

As I began writing my own story and gaining life experience, I began to grasp that I needed to start reprogramming how I perceived myself. In order to heal and find personal happiness,

I needed to forgo the reality my parents lived in and create my own. I learned that I could have value beyond how good I looked in a bathing suit. People actually liked me, and I knew a couple things.

While putting myself through college, I worked at a few makeup counters at Macy's in the mall. I worked with this hilarious woman named Janet who was 30 years my senior but made me laugh like a peer. A fellow coworker was talking with Janet and me about how she felt horrible when she looked in the mirror. Janet said, "Oh, I have the opposite problem. I look in the mirror and think, 'Damn, I look GOOOOOD!' Probably a lot more than I should." This made me laugh, but more importantly, it made me realize that I was secretly like Janet—I've always enjoyed what I saw in the mirror but felt that I wasn't allowed or supposed to like it. I hid my love for my body and my confidence to make other people feel comfortable. But I'm not a couch or a pair of sweatpants—making other people comfortable is not my job, especially if it involves holding back who I really am.

Once I recognized that I was trying to meet the standards of others instead of considering how *I* felt about my body, I was able to begin deleting the negative programming taking up storage on my subconscious hard drive. Ten years later, I'm working as a body-positive stylist helping other women overcome their own body image challenges. I've styled and hosted videos that have gone mega-viral and caught the eye of a Fortune 500 company where I quickly joined the corporate team and helped shape their approach to plus-size fashion. The point? Fuck a hater.

Why We Think We Know What We Think We Know

Confidence can feel like a scarce commodity because we're often made to feel like we don't deserve it unless we "earn it." Before we can love who we are, we're gonna need to find a bunch of other "worthy" people who can validate us first. We're convinced that we just have to become a little bit smarter, skinnier, and more successful before we can actually trust and accept ourselves.

How can you get where you want to go if YOU don't believe in YOU? We all have a bit of "negative programming" that we need to remove from our subconscious hard drive. We often box ourselves in with labels, ideals, and negative self-perception.

You Are What You Think

If we understood the power of our thoughts, we would guard them more closely. If we understood the awesome power of our words, we would prefer silence to almost anything negative. In our thoughts and words, we create our own weaknesses and our own strengths. Our limitations and joys begin in our hearts. We can always replace negative with positive.
—Betty Eadie, author

Words cannot change our reality, but they can change how we perceive reality. The language we choose creates filters through which we view ourselves, obstacles, and opportunities. When we choose words fueled by positivity and gratitude over negativity, we can reprogram the way we view who we are.

YOU'RE NOT AN IMPOSTOR, YOUR IMPOSTOR SYNDROME IS AN IMPOSTOR

Wait, what's impostor syndrome again?

In her paper *The Imposter Phenomenon*, published in *International Journal of Behavioral Science*, clinical psychologist Dr. Jaruwan Sakulku wrote: "Individuals with the Impostor Phenomenon [aka "impostor syndrome"] experience intense feelings that their achievements are undeserved and worry that they are likely to be exposed as a fraud."

Though impostor syndrome isn't a diagnosis listed in the *Diagnostic and Statistical Manual of Mental Disorders*, some psychologists do acknowledge that it is a very real and specific form of intellectual self-doubt. According to the American Psychological Association, impostor syndrome frequently induces anxiety and often depression.

Who suffers from it?

According to the *The Imposter Phenomenon*, an estimated 70 percent of people will experience at least one episode of the impostor phenomenon in their lives. Anyone can view themselves as an impostor if they fail to internalize their success.

This experience is not exclusive to people who are highly successful. Most subsequent research in this area has examined impostor phenomenon as a personality trait or disposition.

How can you combat it?

Researchers have identified a number of contributing factors of impostorism, including perfectionism (this bitch again) and family environment (our subconscious hard drive). Most with impostor syndrome are still able to fulfill their academic or work requirements despite their self-perceived fraudulence.

So how can you fight the feeling that your success is fraudulent or due only to luck? Remind yourself of the following:

YOU ARE NOT ALONE. Many other successful people feel the same way that you do. Serena Williams, Tina Fey, and Maya Angelou are women I admire who have said publicly that they've suffered from impostor syndrome. I like to remind myself that even my own heroes can feel this way despite their abundant successes.

YOU ARE NOT A FRAUD. Look at the facts. When you start to feel self-doubt creeping in, take a moment to reflect on what you have accomplished already.

YOU GOTTA BE BAD TO GET GOOD. Get comfortable with being a student if you want to become a teacher. Adjust your expectations if they don't involve falling and getting back up. This is how growth happens.

Practice Positive Prose

In order to change the way we think and speak about ourselves, we have to . . . change the way we think and speak about ourselves. Over the next 24 hours, I encourage you to observe the language you choose as well as the language of those around you. When you catch yourself being negative or ungrateful, simply practice positivity by rephrasing your words in a productive way.

EXAMPLES

ϟ Instead of saying "I'm such a messy person," try "I'm working on being less messy." One implies defeat, and the other enables growth.

ϟ Swap "I have to go to work" for "I get to go to work." Because, hello, having a job is a blessing.

ϟ Substitute "I prefer to highlight my legs" in place of "I hate the way my arms look." Shaming your body won't change your appearance, but it will affect the way you view yourself.

> **Confidence** (*noun*) Full trust in ourselves or in others' abilities. Accepting our imperfect human nature and loving ourselves regardless
>
> **Ego** (*noun*) Our individual self-esteem or self-importance. The level at which we view our importance
>
> **Egotistical** (*adjective*) Conceited, pretentious, self-centered, annoying AF

Even within the definition, there is a thin line between self-esteem and self-importance when it comes to ego. Confidence is key if you want to achieve something outside your comfort zone; however, a lack of self-awareness can leave blind spots in your life.

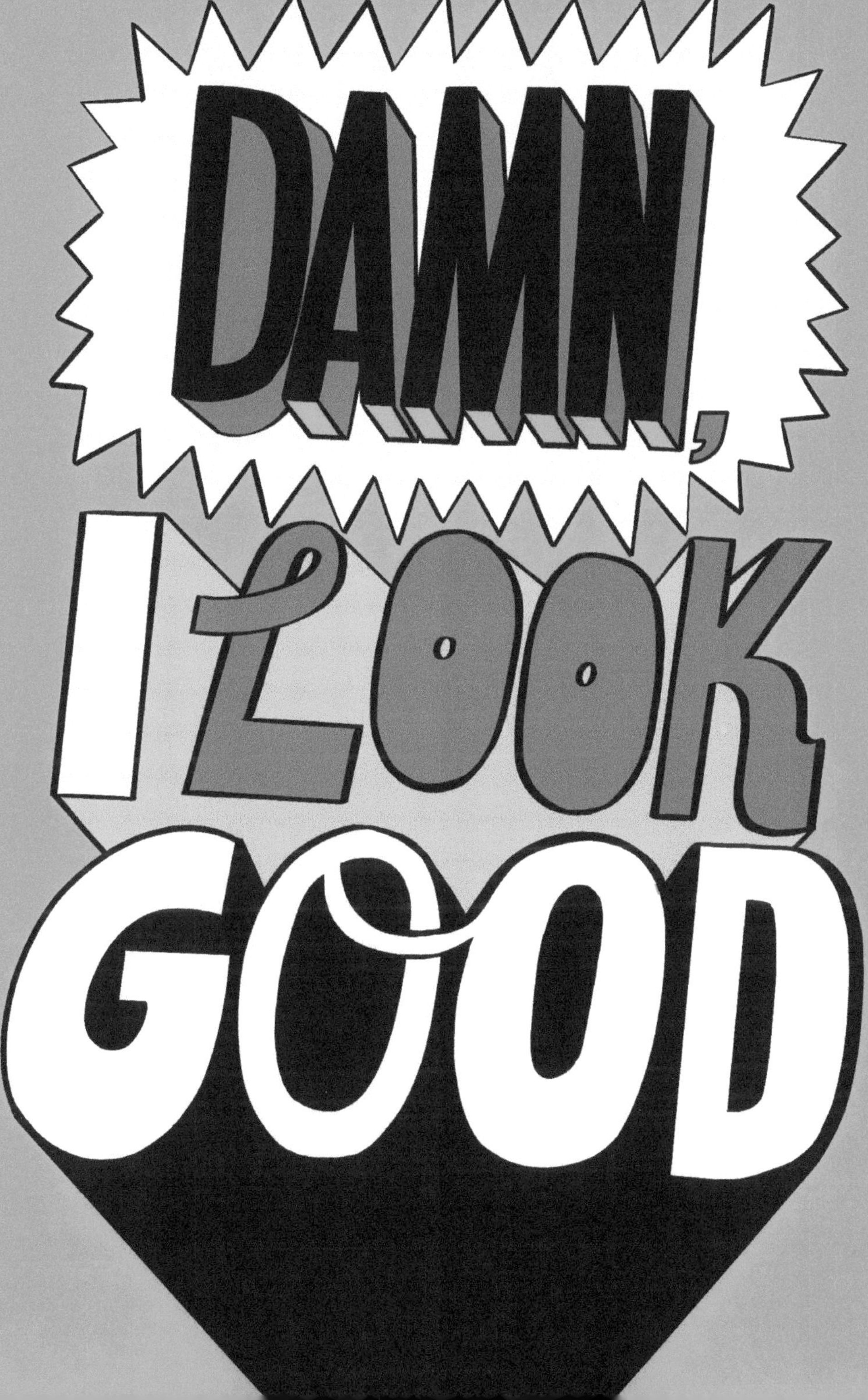
DAMN,
I LOOK
GOOD

DE-FUCK YOUR MIND

Let's pause to reflect on the things you think you know about yourself.

Have you ever thought you couldn't do something based on society's or another person's perception of you?

_____

_____

_____

_____

What are the facts regarding your capabilities, and what is incorrect information you previously accepted as fact?

_____

_____

_____

_____

_____

_____

_____

_____

_____

What ingredients do you think make a strong person?

_____

_____

_____

_____

Do you think of yourself as a strong person? Why or why not?

_____

_____

_____

_____

What is one example of negative language you want to commit to eliminating from your life?

_____

_____

_____

_____

_____

CHAPTER 2

Leggo
My Ego

"The ego hurts you like this: You become
obsessed with the one person who does not love you.
Blind to the rest who do."

—Warsan Shire, author

While confidence is essential for success, ego holds us back when we have an exaggerated sense of our own value or importance. Ego cares what other people think about us because it's looking for validation from others instead of ourselves. Ego looks only for perfection, while confidence accepts that we are not perfect but we're lovable anyway.

Humble Thy Ass

My husband, Michael, is a chef. He graduated top of his class at Le Cordon Bleu, and as his completely unbiased wife, I can tell you with great certainty that he is the best cook in the universe. While working as an executive chef (fancy title for head bitch in charge), he often had to conduct job interviews. One of the questions he would ask those applying for prep cook positions is if they were comfortable washing dishes. All would say yes because, duh. Until one day he was interviewing a recent culinary school graduate who answered, "I went to culinary school. I'm not washing dishes."

Michael explained that the kitchen works as a team and sometimes he, too, must jump in, roll up his sleeves, and wash dishes, if that's what needs to be done. The interviewee had no on-the-job culinary experience, yet his ego kept him from being self-aware enough to see he was placing himself above the customer and the needs of his potential coworkers. He didn't get the job.

Little did he know, my husband started in the kitchen as a prep cook himself, worked his cute ass off, and was promoted to executive chef based on his work ethic a few short months after getting hired (kinda unheard of, TBH).

He got where he was by working hard and doing whatever was needed in every position he held. This helped him leverage each opportunity into a higher rank in the kitchen and a bigger paycheck. As you move up the line, you gain confidence in different skills that you can only learn through experience. This strengthens your confidence steadily. Just because you think you're too good to wash dishes does not actually mean that you are.

Ego may keep you from washing dishes, but it will also probably keep you from getting the job.

Get Comfortable Being Bad At What You Desire to Be Good At

To be courageous, we must be willing to surrender our perfectionism, if only for a moment. If my self-worth is attached to being flawless, why would I ever try to learn anything new? After all, learning requires mistakes.

—*Vironika Tugaleva, author*

> **Perfectionism** (*noun*) Our egotistical hustle to try to convince others and ourselves we are worthy of love and acceptance. An unattainable goal

Perfectionism is the mean girl side of our ego, and she's a fake-ass bitch. You might as well nickname her Regina George. Or Heather. She's always telling you that in order to be liked, you must be perfect. The thing is, perfection isn't even a thing. What is perfect to one person can be terrible to another—it's as subjective as art.

We can get so fixated on wanting to be seen as "right" that we avoid trying new things so we won't feel disappointed or not good enough. The problem is that in order to be great at most things, you must be bad at them first. Don't let perfectionism hustle you out of your potential.

Stop Shaming Yourself for Being Human

Shame corrodes the very part of us that believes we are capable of change.

—Brené Brown, shame researcher and author

> **Shame** (*noun*) The humiliation and/or anxiety and/or sadness that comes from the feeling of being wrong, foolish, imperfect, etc.

Shame is perfectionism and ego's bestie. When these three shrews get together, watch out. They expect us to be the opposite of human—flawless, foolproof, and fake AF. In order to be great, we have to get extra comfy with being "bad" and adjust our expectations.

Expectations are the root of disappointment. Knowing you won't be perfect at something helps alleviate any anxiety your ego might be feeling about not always being right, especially if you were raised in an environment that placed looking and behaving "right" above living authentically.

Being mentally flexible and withholding judgment of yourself will enable you to avoid wasting time and emotional energy that you can instead use to become great. On that same note, those self-deprecating jokes probably aren't helping, either.

Grow Up If You Wanna Glow Up

Becoming is better than being.
—Carol Dweck, professor of psychology

> **Mindset** (*noun*) The attitude with which we think about ourselves, others, and the situations around us
>
> **Fixed mindset** (*noun*) Being shortsighted AF. Being a rigid little bitch. Believing that our capabilities are fixed traits and that "natural talent" or past events dictate our future outcomes
>
> **Growth mindset** (*noun*) The belief that everyone's abilities can be developed through commitment and hard-ass work

Having a growth mindset is imperative for success both professionally and personally. When we are thinking with a growth mindset, we believe that our abilities can be developed through dedication and hard work. This dispels the myth that success comes from luck versus persistence. A growth mindset allows you to see even "failures" as opportunities to get better. A fixed mindset does just that: keeps you exactly where you are.

When I decided I wanted to make a docuseries podcast (which later became *Something Was Wrong*) about emotional abuse, I knew I wouldn't be able to achieve the same audio or production quality with my limited resources and knowledge as huge podcasts with big teams and budgets. But the idea of not making something I knew could help people (and myself) just because it wasn't perfect seemed petty AF to me.

I committed to letting my ideas shine and being vulnerable with my art, even if the delivery wouldn't be perfect. I am forever grateful that I didn't let perfectionism keep me from pursuing something that has been so life-changing for myself and others. With a growth mindset, I'm still pushing myself to get better every day—I'm just giving myself grace in knowing I'm doing the fucking best I can.

I'm a big American football fan (go Niners!). Occasionally, sports announcers will talk about how certain players "play with a chip on their shoulder," which is actually a compliment. It's used to describe a football player who has had a difficult path to reach where they are now. They have used that "underdog" energy to rise to the top and prove those who doubted them wrong.

When we hold ourselves accountable to giving our most sincere efforts, we can sleep well knowing we gave it 100 percent. While talent and "natural ability" are a great start, true success comes from ceaseless effort.

This is how I would describe my own commitment to personal growth. When I doubt myself, instead of letting negativity win, I use it as fuel to further my vision. I turn pain into passion.

Why Compare When You Can Share?

Comparison is an act of violence against the self.
—Iyanla Vanzant, New Thought spiritual teacher, author, and speaker

We're all in luck—success is not pizza. One person having prosperity does not keep another from having their slice, too. Comparison is the thief of joy, energy, and time. Let the success of others motivate and inspire you instead. Focus on your own hustle so intently that you don't have time to be jealous of anyone else's. Why do you think trolls and haters have so much free time to sit on the Internet and talk shit? They're so busy criticizing others that they never have time to work on themselves.

EGO EXORCISM

Let's reflect on how ego and perfectionism have no place in our lives.

Think of a time your ego held you back from personal progress. How can you handle this differently in the future?

_____

_____

_____

When has perfectionism or shame kept you from pursuing your passions in the past? How do you plan to refocus your energy on progress instead?

_____

_____

_____

What's an example of how a growth mindset has aided your success in the past?

_____

_____

_____

CHAPTER

3

All You Need Is Self-Love

> "Love yourself first and everything else falls into line. You really have to love yourself to get anything done in this world."
>
> —Lucille Ball, actor, comedian, and producer

> **Self-care** (*noun*) The care of ourselves without the
> assistance of others. Prioritization of our needs
>
> **Self-image** (*noun*) The way we see ourselves. The ideas
> we have about who we are
>
> **Self-talk** (*noun*) The language and manner we use to talk
> to ourselves

Our self-image has been slowly formed through our experiences, culture, family, and environment. Though some might feel positive self-talk comes naturally to them, many of us have learned to be hypercritical of ourselves through the lens of societal expectations, complicated family dynamics, and/or mental health challenges.

Researchers at the American Psychological Association have found that it's not just about what you say to yourself, it's also the language that you use to say it. If you are struggling to speak kindly to yourself, research indicates that speaking to or about yourself in the third person can be helpful. Using third-person self-talk can help you step back and observe your emotions instead of making emotion-fueled decisions. It can also help you reduce stress and anxiety.

Our negative self-talk (aka our inner hater) can become so loud that our inner cheerleader becomes difficult to hear. It is essential to remember that how we speak to ourselves matters. But there are ways to give that cheerleader a megaphone and tell the hater to fuck right off.

Thankfully, self-image is something we can constantly improve. It's dynamic and ever-evolving. A healthy self-image starts with learning to unconditionally accept and love who we are now.

You Talkin' to You?

As hard as it is, owning who you are and knowing what you want is the only sure path to affirmation . . . I want women to know they can get out of any situation if they return to their core source of strength: themselves.

—Ashley Graham, model and body positivity advocate

If negative self-talk is something that you (also) struggle with, affirmations are a great way to remind yourself how fucking great you are. Scientific research has revealed that repeating affirmations multiple times in a day can slowly start developing a sense of belief in those words (Steele, 1988). Affirmations help remind us who we are and where we are going, so be your own hype (wo)man.

I like to convert my own negative self-talk into affirmations. This helps me target specific thoughts I'm overcoming. Here are some examples of how you can acknowledge your feelings and turn them into positive affirmations:

⚠ **NEGATIVE THOUGHT**: You've peaked professionally and should just be happy you've gotten to where you are now.

♡ **AFFIRMATION**: My achievements have come from my hard work and unique vision. I am proud of myself. My journey is just beginning.

⚠ **NEGATIVE THOUGHT**: I'm so unhealthy. I made terrible choices today.

♡ **AFFIRMATION**: I am full of loving and healthy thoughts that eventually convert into my life experiences. I am in control of the choices I make.

Be Your Own Self-Care Bear

Caring for myself is not self-indulgence, it is self-preservation, and that is an act of political warfare.
—Audre Lorde, *activist, poet, and essayist*

Self-care is an essential piece of loving ourselves. Those of us with mental health challenges often struggle to take care of even our most basic needs when we are swept up in an undertow of depression or drowning in anxiety. Self-care looks different for everyone; simply prioritize an area in which you feel you deserve more attention.

The relationship we have with ourselves is the most important relationship of our lifetime. There's a reason we have to put our oxygen mask on first before we can help others. We can't help others if we're dying.

WHAT SELF-CARE CAN LOOK LIKE

- Prioritizing daily hygiene (brushing your teeth, taking a shower, etc.)
- Not putting off going to the doctor/therapist/dentist
- Saying no to something you don't have the time or energy for
- Spending time with a loved one
- Going to bed early
- Taking a walk
- Making time for self-reflection/journaling/meditation
- Volunteering for a cause you are passionate about
- Cleaning your room

Mindfulness for a Mind Full of Mess

Sometimes you need to sit lonely on the floor in a quiet room in order to hear your own voice and not let it drown in the noise of others.

—Charlotte Eriksson, author and songwriter

> **Mindfulness** *(noun)* Being present in our current moment in time. Focusing our attention on what's happening IRL

Half of my productivity struggle is staying mindful and focused on the task at hand. Between life, social media, my insanely loud family, and anxiety, there are lots of distractions. When it's time to work, I have learned that I must create an environment that supports my mission—one that allows me to be hyper-focused on the hustle at hand. For me, this means scheduling time that I know I will be able to be completely focused without any interruptions. Ironically, I was struggling to get writing done for this book, so I booked an Airbnb yurt in the middle of the woods to ensure my focus wasn't divided.

Mindfulness is not about oil diffusers and anxiety apps. Trust me, I'm anything but calm. Mindfulness is the psychological process of consciously bringing our attention to the present moment. It is something I still must actively work at, but I have found a few ways to set myself up for success before I begin my work:

Put your stupid phone away! No, for real. If you want to listen to music, put that timewaster in airplane mode and turn it upside down. Yes, it's tempting to go on Pinterest right now and pretend you're ever gonna make any of that ridiculousness, but now IS. NOT. THE. TIME.

Create a checklist for each work session. Even if you only have an hour, take one minute to draft a practical list of actionable tasks you can and will achieve. This not only helps us stay on task, but also helps support our confidence in ourselves and our ability to get shit done. Plus, it's fun to cross things off a list.

Set yourself up for success. Know yourself. If you notice you sometimes struggle to remember things (same), set electronic reminders, keep a log of your progress, and use a calendar to track your meetings and deadlines.

Through trial and error, find what works best for you to feel the most focused and engaged.

MINDFULNESS PRACTICE: BODY SCAN

A common mindfulness strategy is called body scanning. This technique is used to help us connect with our physical bodies and refocus our minds. Thirty minutes is the recommended time to allow for this practice, but if that isn't feasible, use whatever time you do have. You can lie down or sit up if you fall asleep easily. Ready? Follow these simple steps:

Close your eyes. If you prefer, you can lower or half-close your eyelids instead.

Take deep breaths. Begin by focusing simply on breathing in and out. As you breathe, think about relaxing each part of your body, starting with your head. If you are interested in specific breathing methods, I recommend the 4-7-8 breathing technique—breathing in through the nose for four seconds, holding the breath for seven seconds, and exhaling out of the mouth for eight seconds.

Feel the feels. What sensations do you have? Do you feel any tingling, pressure, tightness, temperature, or buzzing within your body? Perhaps you feel simply neutral—that's great, too. Just focus on feeling what comes naturally without judgment.

Continue to refocus yourself. If you've started thinking about what you need from the grocery store, don't worry. Gently remind yourself to redirect your focus to your breathing. Think of this exercise as training—not forcing.

You did it! Once you have scanned your body from head to toe and explored your sensations, take a few minutes to focus on your body as a whole. Feel your entire body breathing effortlessly and naturally. If your eyes have been closed, slowly open them and take in your environment.

Shake It Off, Drop It Like It's Hot, Just Give It the Boot

We have important goals to reach, so we don't have any more time for negative self-talk, fear of the unknown, or the distractions around us. You cannot get better in the environment that made you sick, and you sure as hell can't reach your highest potential with negativity. Gather up all that trash talk and burn it in a dumpster fire. Turn the ashes into a face mask and let's glow the fuck up.

Observing ourselves from the third person or an outsider's perspective can be highly effective for fighting negative self-talk. Practice speaking to yourself the same way you would a friend, child, or partner. Consider how the people you love would speak to you and what they would say to encourage you.

If you're still struggling with your inner critic (because you're a human and not a robot), reach out to a loved one who has seen you at your best and your worst in life. Tell them what your challenges and goals are and ask them if they have any words of encouragement for you. It's completely okay to let people who love you know that you would like specific emotional support when you need it. After all, wouldn't you do the same for them? Strong people are smart enough to ask for help.

Leave Negative Self-Talk on Read

Negative self-talk doesn't just magically disappear the day we decide to unapologetically love ourselves. It's a continuous journey of self-acceptance, and battling negative self-talk is the perfect way to tell our inner critic to GTFO.

The way we talk about and to ourselves influences our energy and vibrations.

Here are some examples of how a growth mindset can aid us in fighting negative self-talk and a fixed mindset.

⚠ **NEGATIVE SELF-TALK**: "I can't believe I forgot to mail my taxes. I'm such a moron. I fuck everything up. Why can't I ever get my shit together? Fuck it, I can't deal with this right now."

♡ **GROWTH MINDSET**: "Welp, that was a big screw-up. In the future, I'm going to prioritize getting my taxes in earlier. Lesson learned!"

⚠ **NEGATIVE SELF-TALK**: "I posted my new website, and no one liked or commented on my Instagram post. Everyone must hate me and my website."

♡ **GROWTH MINDSET**: "If I want people to see my website, I'll probably need to find creative ways to share it. I should research the best time of the week to share posts like this on my feed and new ways to create engagement."

⚠ **NEGATIVE SELF-TALK**: "I feel like I'm always broke and can never get caught up on my bills. I hate being an adult."

♡ **GROWTH MINDSET**: "I want to find new ways to save money and create a budget so I can feel less anxiety about my finances."

WHO DO YOU THINK YOU ARE?

It's time for reflection and some humble braggage.

What do your loved ones think about you? How would they describe you to a stranger? What value do they see in you, and how do they encourage you to be great?

_____

_____

_____

Describe yourself in three sentences.

_____

_____

_____

Where did these ideas come from?

_____

_____

_____

Who does your best friend think you are?

_____

_____

_____

EVERYONE ELSE'S PERCEPTION IS JUST AS SUBCONSCIOUSLY SKEWED AS YOURS

Now it's time to write down how you see your best friend. Then reflect on how your BFF would describe themselves, both similarly and in contrast. (I triple dog dare you to ask your friend to do the activity with you sometime as well. Both of you write down how you view each other and then how you see yourselves. Also maybe give them a copy of this book if they wrote down super-harsh stuff about themselves.)

How would you describe your best friend to a stranger?

_____

_____

_____

How would your bestie describe themselves?

_____

_____

_____

MENTAL HEALTH CHECK-IN

"We need to learn to identify the signs of mental-health issues. We need to have the courage to reach out and have tough conversations with our friends and family members—and get help ourselves when we need it."

—Michelle Obama, lawyer, author, producer, and former First Lady

Depression (*noun*) A sometimes soul-sucking empty feeling of emotional dead inside-ness. Prolonged feelings of sadness that make you want to withdraw from life, isolate yourself to your bed, and watch mindless TV while you shovel cookie dough into your mouth

Mental health (*noun*) 1. Our psychological wellness, health, strength. The quality in which we navigate life and all its fuckery 2. The area of psychology that studies how TF we are handling life

I want to take a moment to talk about the importance of caring for our mental health. This is another way we can take exquisite care of ourselves. Sometimes depression doesn't "look" like depression at first glance. It can feel confusing—are you depressed or just in a funk?

We often associate being depressed with feeling extremely sad. Being sad is an emotion, and depression is a medical condition (aka a mood disorder).

I'm not a doctor or a therapist, so I look to the experts for advice when it comes to mental health. The renowned Mayo Clinic states that although depression may occur only once during your life, people typically have multiple depressive episodes.

Symptoms of Depression

- Feelings of sadness, tearfulness, emptiness, or hopelessness
- Angry outbursts, irritability, or frustration, even over small matters
- Loss of interest or pleasure in most or all normal activities, such as sex, hobbies, or sports
- Sleep disturbances, including insomnia or sleeping too much
- Tiredness and lack of energy, so even small tasks take extra effort
- Reduced appetite and weight loss or increased cravings for food and weight gain
- Anxiety, agitation, or restlessness
- Slowed thinking, speaking, or body movements
- Feelings of worthlessness or guilt, fixating on past failures, or self-blame
- Trouble thinking, concentrating, making decisions, and remembering things
- Frequent or recurrent thoughts of death, suicidal thoughts, suicide attempts, or suicide
- Unexplained physical problems, such as back pain or headaches

(Source: Mayo Clinic)

If you are thinking about suicide, are worried about a friend or loved one, or would like emotional support, please call the **National Suicide Prevention Lifeline at 1-800-273-8255**. If you think you're suffering from depression, talk to your doctor and please check out the free mental health resources in the back of this book.

Over the past year or so of my research for my podcast and through therapy, I have learned so much about myself. The more I learn, the more compassion I give myself, which is truly life-changing. Learning to first accept and love ourselves is clichéd as hell but true AF.

I'm painfully aware that therapy can be costly and perhaps even a little intimidating, but as a survivor of trauma, I can tell you it can be life-changing. Thankfully, there are also so many free in-person and online support groups out there. Check out the resources section at the end of the book for more info. I've attended in-person and online therapy depending on my needs. PsychologyToday.com has a free search tool that allows you to easily find a counselor based on your needs.

If you suffer from anxiety, depression, PTSD, or any other psychological challenges, please know that this book is absolutely still for you. In fact, it's written by someone with all three, so *twinning*. Our pasts do not define us or dictate our importance. We can choose to turn pain into passion and make magic with it.

> **Rut** (*noun*) Feeling stale, bored, unsettled, uninspired, or rigid

Different from depression, being in a rut is a stale, stagnant, bored feeling. I'm personally in a funk when I'm uninspired or burnt out and in need of a break. So how can you shake off this fixed mindset and get back to the business of being awesome as hell?

Tips for Being Less of a Dick to Yourself and Breaking Out of a Rut

LET GO OF PAST MISTAKES AND REGRETS. We often feel uninspired when we are in a negative self-talk cycle. Gently remind yourself that spending time in the past only subtracts from the time you could be investing in yourself.

ASSESS YOUR ENVIRONMENT. What cultivates a productive environment for you? If your current surroundings aren't inspiring you, change things up. If you work remotely, try working from a coffee shop or quiet space that motivates you.

INSPIRE YOURSELF. Sometimes we can get so lost in our heads that we forget how far we've come and where we're heading. Need an inspo boost? Try creating a goal/inspo board or mission statement or appreciating the work of someone who inspires you (without comparing yourself).

What Other People Think of You Is None of Your Damn Business

> "Life is too short to waste any amount of time on wondering what other people think about you. In the first place, if they had better things going on in their lives, they wouldn't have the time to sit around and talk about you. What's important to me is not others' opinions of me, but what's important to me is my opinion of myself."
>
> —C. JoyBell C., author

> **Self-perception** (*noun*) How you see yourself and your individual impact. Self-awareness

Self-perception (aka self-awareness) helps us view our impact in the world. Our actions, thoughts, and beliefs assemble into two major elements of who we are—our ego and our true self. Separating our ego from our true self is the first step toward understanding our environment and our individual impact within it. Self-awareness also helps us recognize our strengths, even when others don't. Recognizing our own value pushes us to advocate properly for our needs.

Ego and shame try to tell us that we need the approval of others in order to accept ourselves, but we don't. Ego may help you fit in, but self-love helps you stand out. Go ahead and let self-love punch ego and shame right in the face.

How can your unique vision shine if you're busy imitating someone else's? Spoiler alert: It can't. Which is why one of the best gifts you can give yourself is knowing who you are and not giving two fucks about what other people think.

Vulnerability Is Powerful, Also Scary

Owning our story can be hard but not nearly as difficult as spending our lives running from it. Embracing our vulnerabilities is risky but not nearly as dangerous as giving up on love and belonging and joy—the experiences that make us the most vulnerable. Only when we are brave enough to explore the darkness will we discover the infinite power of our light.
—Brené Brown, shame researcher and author

> **Vulnerability** (*noun*) The act of being open and exposing
> your authentic self and beliefs to others, despite the
> possibility that others may judge or harm you

Sharing our passion with the world can be one of the scariest yet most rewarding things we do. Our ego and inner hater wants us to believe that we should avoid taking risks because it will help us avoid the shame that comes from others criticizing us. We don't want to risk being seen as "wrong" or "different" or "weird" or whatever.

As anxiety-inducing as sharing our authentic self/art/ideas may be, the pros outweigh the cons. When we choose to allow others to see who we genuinely are, our vulnerability opens them up to feeling comfortable doing the same. This helps us surround ourselves with other real people and build trustworthy relationships. Don't get me wrong; some people will hate you, but that will likely have very little to do with you and more to do with their own journey.

As a recovering people-pleaser who makes a living on the Internet, ignoring negativity and trusting my unique vision is my kryptonite. When *Something Was Wrong* first released, the first 200-ish reviews on iTunes were so positive, supportive, and kind. This is likely because 100 percent of them were from people who knew me.

As my podcast's success spread, the reviews from haters started to flow in. I told myself I wouldn't read them. Then I did. Then I cried. I put my heart and soul into this project for months and felt so defeated by the opinions of a handful of people. I let the minority of people who didn't like something I said or did take away from the thousands of people who loved it. I wasn't focusing my energy on my work or gratitude for my achievements. I was wasting it on what other people thought. My ego was hurt.

I began obsessing about how to make these people understand me—to the point that I was losing sleep and no longer enjoying something I was previously so passionate about. My husband, Michael, gave me almost daily pep talks (sorry about that, boo). I was so focused on the negativity that I was keeping myself from internalizing my success.

Finally, I made the decision to let go of the idea that I could make everyone like me. I started creating boundaries with the Internet and myself. Within a week of this separation, I started feeling excited by my work again. My work (and anxiety) benefited from creating this boundary. The more I honor my vision and purpose, the happier I feel.

They say you haven't really made it until you've got haters—so if you do, welcome to the club. Try to refocus your energy away from their negativity as much as possible. Your work is your art, an extension of you—and you can't account for taste.

You are the only you in this universe, and that is your superpower. No matter what kind of goals you have, it is vital that your creation showcases who YOU are and what YOUR unique vision is. Don't let the opinions of basic trolls subtract from what you're accomplishing. Vulnerability enables creativity, growth, and trust within ourselves. You think the trolls are out there turning their vulnerability into power? Psh, doubt it.

Speak and Act Responsibly: The Rest Is Out of Your Control

We cannot (and should not) control what other people think of us, the choices we make . . . or the self-help books we read. Anyone who has that ability is basically a supervillain with mind control. If you attempt to make everyone happy, you will end up making no one happy, even yourself. And guess what? IT. WON'T. MATTER. People are going to love you. People are going to hate you. Be true to yourself and your work will benefit. Do not be so afraid of vulnerability and shame that you hold yourself back from getting where you desire to be.

Get Feedback from People Who Actually Know What They're Talking About

So how can we sync up our ego and self-awareness? This is where the value of feedback from trusted people comes in. In order to avoid blind spots in our personal growth, relationships, and goal-getting, we need to gather feedback from mentors/ experts who are knowledgeable and experienced.

For example, if you want to write a cookbook, don't ask your best friend what she thinks of your recipes, unless your BFF happens to be a chef. Find a culinary professional with a background in writing cookbooks. They'll be able to provide you with realistic, on-the-job advice that will aid in reaching your goals.

Feedback is no longer beneficial when we take the advice of those who are not qualified to give it. Our vision gets cloudy, and we don't feel the same satisfaction as when we trust ourselves and create genuinely. This includes haters, trolls, Internet reviewers, and even well-meaning friends and family. As *New York Times* best-selling author Simone Elkeles so eloquently put it, "Opinions are like assholes, everybody's got one and everyone thinks everyone else's stinks."

I have discovered it's imperative for me to create boundaries between myself and reading things like public reviews or comments about my work on iTunes, Amazon, and social media as much as possible. This does not make me a weaker person or less of a boss, or limit my passion or growth. It does enable me to focus solely on my work at hand and my unique vision.

The Only Truth Is What's True for You

Once you have been working toward your goals for a while, it can be tempting to compare your "success" to others' in your industry/arena. This is a pointless, time-wasting, fruitless venture. Other people's accomplishments in no way hinder your ability to meet your goals. Supporting others who work in your field empowers both of you simultaneously. Being happy for someone else costs you nothing. Celebrating the achievements of others fosters an abundance mentality and growth mindset in your industry.

Conversely, other people comparing themselves to you and your accomplishments is not your problem. It is not your job to make other people comfortable with your success. Those who truly love you will be happy for your advancement without feeling the need to criticize you or make it about them. If you find that you have people in your life who seem to be interested in every detail of your failures but barely congratulate your success, they are probably not your friends.

vulnerability IS SCARY and WORTH it.

PART II

FALLING MADLY IN LOVE WITH YOURSELF #1

SELF LOVE

You are the CEO, president, financial officer, all the VPs, and the board of your own fan club in life. No one else is in the business of you but you. I tell myself, "You are in the Tiffany Reese business. You are the one who has to prioritize what is the wisest and most beneficial thing for Tiffany Reese." This helps me observe my opportunities from a bird's-eye view and not get caught up in the emotion of decisions. It helps me avoid selling myself short or accepting work I don't care about because I worry it will be my last offer ever. This is especially essential if you plan to be self-employed. If we don't pay our own rates, no one else will either.

The best way to teach others how we deserve to be treated is through the way we love ourselves. The same can be said for the way we assess our worth and decide who gains access to our life. We cannot reach our fullest potential unless we value who we are and what we bring to the table. Odds are you bring some pretty rad shit to the table.

Life is too short to waste hating and shaming who we are. Yet everywhere we look, there are new ways to feel shitty and devalued. Social media and reality TV haven't helped. We must be resilient and commit to loving ourselves unapologetically and assertively.

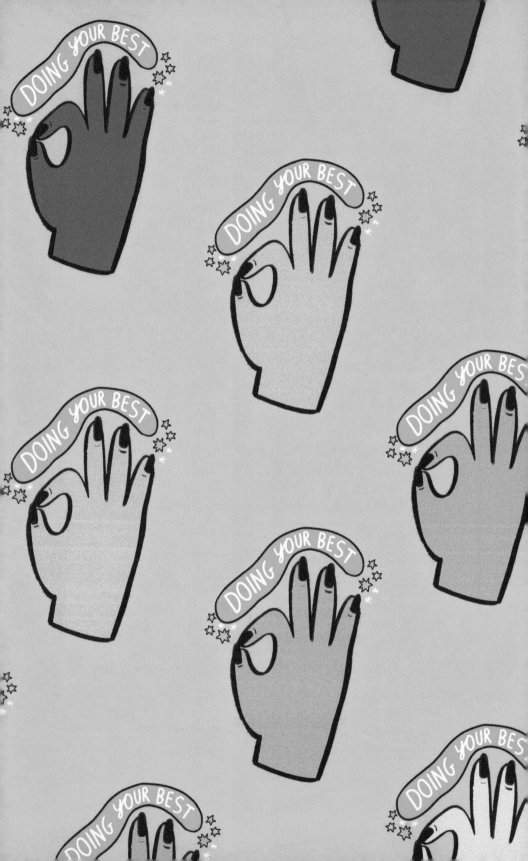

Find Faith in Something AND Zen the Fuck Out

> "Believe something and the Universe is on its way to being changed. Because you've changed, by believing. Once you've changed, other things start to follow. Isn't that the way it works?"
>
> —*Diane Duane*, So You Want to Be a Wizard

> **Faith** (*noun*) Unconditional belief in and trust in something or someone

A belief in a higher power is important because having faith in something bigger than ourselves can help us find peace and feel a connection that we share with all living things. If you're not a "person of faith," you probably feel kinda awkward right now. Don't worry, this isn't necessarily about believing in *that* kind of higher power. Faith is simply a belief in a power greater than ourselves.

You Gotta Have Faith . . . in What Is Up to You

Believe in crystals, Keanu Reeves, Labradoodles, or just yourself. It's the actual faith that's important. Gratitude reminds us of what we have already been blessed with, while faith inspires hopefulness for our future.

There's a lot of scary shit happening in the world, and I have no idea why bad stuff happens. I do know, however, that faith sustains us during our darkest hours. I'm not one of those everything-happens-for-a-reason people as much as I am a make-the-best-out-of-whatcha-got-and-have-faith-in-yourself kinda gal.

Having faith manifests feelings of positivity, hope, and purpose. When in doubt, have faith in yourself and tell your rude-ass anxiety to quiet down. It's time to start believing in things you can't see (yet) and trust they are out there waiting for you.

Abundance Mentality: Happiness Isn't Pizza—There's Enough for Everyone

An abundance mentality springs from internal security, not from external rankings, comparisons, opinions, possessions, or associations.

—Stephen Covey, author and educator

> **Abundance mentality** (*noun*) The ideology that there is enough success, love, and opportunities to go around for everyone
>
> **Scarcity mindset** (*noun*) The belief that someone else having something will keep others from having it

American author and businessman Stephen Covey coined the term "abundance mentality" (or "abundance mindset") in his 1989 best-selling book *The 7 Habits of Highly Effective People.* Since then, abundance mentality has been established as beneficial in cultivating personal and spiritual growth.

Having an abundance mentality recognizes that there is enough happiness and success to go around. A scarcity mindset believes that one person having something takes away from another.

When we think with an abundance mindset, the world offers us limitless possibilities. What's not to like?

EMOTIONAL BENEFITS OF AN ABUNDANCE MENTALITY

- Radiating happiness despite circumstances
- Feeling plentiful, imaginative, resourceful
- Envisioning a limitless and satisfying life
- Recognizing opportunities for growth
- Encouraging others and self
- Fostering our faith in our environment and opportunities
- Leveraging others' success as inspiration

Serenity Now!

I'm not religious, but I do pray. It's 60 seconds of meditation, visualizing myself, looking at myself, and being conscious of my own consciousness. That will align me for the rest of the day.

—RuPaul, drag queen, singer, and TV personality

> **Meditate** (*verb*) Focusing our attention inward, thinking deeply

How exhausting is it to think all the time? Let's give that gorgeous brain of yours a break. Not only is meditation a great excuse to close your eyes (as if I need one), it's also scientifically proven to benefit your mental and physical health. Think of meditation as mental hygiene on your self-care list.

BENEFITS OF MEDITATION

- Increases immune function
- Decreases pain and inflammation
- Boosts happiness levels
- Decreases depression, anxiety, and stress

⚡ Increases social connection and emotional intelligence

⚡ Improves your ability to regulate your emotions

⚡ Changes your brain (for the better) and increases gray matter (also a good thing, apparently)

⚡ Increases your focus, multitasking abilities, and memory

⚡ Improves your ability to be creative and think outside the box

Appreciate All the Shit You Have Survived

Being grateful all the time isn't easy. But it's when you feel least thankful that you are most in need of what gratitude can give you: perspective. Gratitude can transform any situation. It alters your vibration, moving you from negative energy to positive. It's the quickest, easiest, most powerful way to effect change in your life—this I know for sure.

—*Oprah Winfrey*, **What I Know for Sure**

> **Gratitude** (*noun*) The art of being thankful for all that you already have in life. Celebrating the ways in which we are blessed and showing true appreciation

Those who have my first book, *Everything Sucks: A Gratitude Journal for People Who Have Been Through Some Sh*t*, know that I am a total slut for gratitude.

Thankfulness helps us see that for every loss, there is also gain, and that with every difficult season in life comes a time for healing and redemption. Gratitude for our personal gifts is highly important and can be beneficial when you're trying to pull yourself out of a self-hatred spiral. Remember, we cannot overcome impostorism if we do not allow ourselves to fully appreciate our success.

Like meditation, practicing gratitude is scientifically linked to improving both our psychological and physical health.

GRATITUDE GAINS

- ⚡ Improves relationships
- ⚡ Strengthens our physical health
- ⚡ Enhances empathy and reduces anger
- ⚡ Strengthens self-confidence
- ⚡ Improves psychological health and mental strength
- ⚡ Increases relaxation and sleep

Want to up your gratitude game? Take two minutes a day to write down three things that you are thankful for. Insert another shameless plug for my book *Everything Sucks: A Gratitude Journal for People Who Have Been Through Some Sh*t* here. But seriously, you can write these things down on a sanitary napkin for all I care. Just taking time to celebrate the gifts the day has given you is so beneficial.

My family likes to practice gratitude collectively. On the nights we all actually make it to the dinner table at the same time, we go around the table and share our highs and lows of the day. This is something we started two years ago, and our whole family (and dinner guests) enjoys acknowledging the best and worst parts of the day. Our rules are simple: You can share unlimited "highs" but only one "low." Parents in the crowd—trust me on this one.

Let Gratitude BE YOUR Attitude

LET YOUR VALUES GUIDE YOU

If an opportunity is not aligned with what matters most to you (your core values), let it pass. The opportunities that don't make your soul sing, or that you can't be excited about, just end up taking space where a better opportunity could be. Don't settle for something fine—wait for something great!
—Leanne Jacobs, **Beautiful Money**

> **Values** (*verb*) Our core beliefs that comprise who we are and what is important to us. Things we believe deeply in and consider important in life

Recognizing what's important to us helps us define our personal values. Some of my personal values are kindness, honesty, trust, accountability, vulnerability, authenticity, positivity, inclusivity, equality, and humor. Once we know what we stand for, we know what we won't put up with, either. This concept has been so healing for me when considering whom I want in my life and how I want to focus my energy.

What values are most important to you?

_____
_____
_____
_____
_____

**If you had to write a mission statement
for who you are, what would it be?**

_____
_____
_____
_____
_____

**What do you want your "work" to say
about you as a person?**

_____
_____
_____
_____
_____

Be Your Own Soulmate

"'Cause I'm my own soulmate

I know how to love me

I know that I'm always gonna hold me down

Yeah, I'm my own soulmate

No, I'm never lonely

I know I'm a queen, but I don't need no crown

Look up in the mirror like 'Damn, she the one'"

—Lizzo, "Soulmate"

> **Soulmate** (*noun*) A being that is flawlessly suited to be in a relationship with another

What if we treated ourselves with the same love, admiration, and compassion we gave our friends? Can you imagine what we could accomplish?! Conversely, if we did talk to our friends the same way we spoke to ourselves, we probably wouldn't have many.

Loving who we are is an inside job, and how we speak about and to ourselves is extremely important. That's why dismissing negative self-talk and focusing on having a growth mindset are so important. Positive energy allows for a more productive and creative lifestyle.

Only You Define You

If I based my love for myself on the words and behaviors of my parents growing up, I'd still be dead inside. But even as a kid, I knew that I was beautiful, smart, loving, silly, and creative. Though it's endlessly painful to have those who are supposed to love you the most in this world treat you like shit, I think even then I knew their cruelty had much more to do with them than it did with me. Not that it makes it hurt less, but it does help me understand that they were wrong.

I was told that I wasn't pretty, that I'd never have a boyfriend or get married because I was too fat. That people were only my friends because they felt sorry for me. If I would just lose weight and act a certain way, I could finally be attractive. I was called names, slapped, punched, scratched, and belittled.

Because my father was a grifter and a sociopath, we moved a lot. Like, every other year. This meant being the fat new girl in school a lot. When I started getting closer to junior high, it was survival mode each day. I was shit on at home and crapped on at school.

My parents put me in Catholic school for seventh grade. They were under the impression that children at private school were nicer so I'd have a better chance of making a friend. They were wrong.

I'll never forget the day the hottest guy in seventh grade, Brett, slipped me a piece of folded paper at school and told me to call him that night. At first I thought, *Finally someone who appreciates this big beautiful ass!* I climbed into the car, opened the note, and read "1-800-94-Jenny." For those who don't know, this was the number (and catchy-ass jingle) for Jenny Craig, a popular weight-loss business in the '90s. I was humiliated and mortified. Another time, he taped a "wide load" sign to my back. Really quality guy, obvz.

At the end of eighth grade, we had a graduation picnic. A popular girl named Maggie and her boyfriend played volleyball with me at said picnic and finally figured out I was funny AF. Maggie and I ended up becoming friends that summer, and it definitely helps when the queen of eighth grade (also the only one who knew how to do her makeup) thinks you're a good time.

Once I did start to make a few friends, I realized how badly I wanted to have boyfriends like they did. However, because I had always been told what a piece of disgusting fat garbage I was, I didn't think I had anything to offer. Being the fat girl during the low-rise jeans, Britney Spears, heroin chic days of the '90s didn't help.

My mother always encouraged me to skip meals, and I knew being fat was "wrong," but because I was a child, I had no idea how I could actually change the fact that I was overweight. My parents placed me in double binds, constantly criticizing my size and then serving me unhealthy foods and desserts all the time. One day I asked my mom how many calories a day I should eat if I wanted to lose weight. Her face lit up like it was Christmas morning and someone finally gave her the skinny cheerleading daughter she'd always wanted. She told me it was best, of course, to eat as little as possible. She then recommended I start at 1,000 calories and work my way down from there. I trusted her and thought, okay, this is what I need to do—eat as little as possible for as long as possible, work out every day, and then I will get skinny and everyone will think I'm hot and valuable and people will hopefully stop taping "wide load" signs to my ass.

Through these methods of starvation, during the summer between freshman and sophomore years of high school, I lost about 75 pounds. As I put on my sneakers each day, my parents would praise me and tell me (finally) how proud they were of me. I became addicted to this feeling and never wanted it to go away. Suddenly people were complimenting me and telling me I looked good. Okay, I thought, *this* is how I get people to love me.

Since I'd lost weight and started gaining value to them, my parents rewarded me by letting me get my belly button pierced (I had to lose 50 pounds first, of course) and attend the local public high school instead of private school. In public school, I learned that boys were much more open about how horny and disgusting they were. And another great way to get validation was to be a "slut." Since all that mattered to me during this phase was being attractive and making sure the opposite sex thought I was hot, being a slut was a natural fit. (That's what she said.) While exploring your sexuality isn't inherently bad (no slut shaming here), I was driven by external validation, and I wasn't doing it for me. Boys did ask me out, but as it turns out, dating high school boys is not always a win.

My mom encouraged this—she even told me on my way to school one morning that I had pretty decent legs now and could stand to make my skirts a bit shorter. After all, gotta make sure I keep attracting dudes—my highest priority in life.

Shortly after my 16th birthday, my dad had to run from the cops or the FBI or something, so we moved to another city, and I was alone again. I tried attending a new high school, but I just didn't connect with people my age. They all seemed to have things like parents who loved them and real childhoods, and I just couldn't relate.

I transferred to homeschool, graduated my sophomore year, got a full-time job, and started creating my exit strategy from my family.

Eventually, I moved into junior college dorms hours away and began experiencing what life could be like away from my family. My 16-year-old-in-junior-college self was also pretty self-destructive. I figured I'd probably kill myself or be killed at some point, so it didn't much matter. I drank excessively, put myself in extremely dangerous situations, and generally didn't give any fucks.

The thing about growing up in toxicity is that it's all you know, so toxicity is normalized. And because I had no outside family, long-term friendships, or support outside myself, I didn't have any clue what a healthy relationship with others or myself looked like. I didn't even understand that this was something I could make better. I just knew I hated my life, I hated myself, and, by my toxic standards, I could really stand to lose another 50 pounds.

As I transitioned from teenage to college Tiffany, I reconnected with my old pal Maggie (the popular girl from Christian school) and told her how miserable I was (probably on AIM chat). Her mom heard I was living on my own at 17, and they invited me to come live with them.

This was the first time I lived somewhere that I actually felt safe. I got a pretty serious boyfriend and figured out there were many other people who thought this wide-load ass looked pretty good in jeans, too.

That boyfriend-turned-fiancé-turned-ex-fiancé opened my eyes to the fact that I was attractive and could be loved. The problem was that I didn't really know what love was supposed to look like. I thought he was my one and only shot at being loved, and when we broke up, I thought for sure I should just go ahead and kill myself. Thankfully, I didn't. Instead, I started working on myself and getting help. I realized that if I wanted to be happy and enjoy my life, I was the only one who could make that happen. I had to be my own soulmate.

I started doing really well in college when I started studying something I was passionate about: fashion. As I gained more life experience, I started to become more secure in showing the confidence I had secretly stored in myself. I began celebrating who I was little by little. I started dating my now-husband, Michael, who taught me a lot about real love, support, and valuing myself.

I began separating myself more and more from my parents' emotional, physical, and substance abuse. I started surrounding myself with people who loved me and spent my energy investing in myself. I began to learn what it felt like to be happy-ish. I opened up to new friends (who have now become my chosen family) and let myself be loved.

I started attending Al-Anon support groups. These are free public support groups for people who are in relationships (or were previously) with alcoholics and addicts. I learned so much about myself through these meetings, but most importantly, I discovered I was not alone. I felt so validated, and that was extremely healing for me. I knew that I didn't want to be a victim of my circumstances anymore. I wanted to be a survivor.

Michael and I got married in 2008 (I was 22, he was 23), and six months later I was hungover, peeing on a stick. Turns out that vodka I drank at Christmas really got the job done. I was pregnant with our firstborn, a boy, whom we later named Jude. This is when I really began my transformation.

When Jude entered our world, I experienced a new kind of love that saturated every part of my soul. I knew the moment he was born that Michael and I would never be the same. I was no longer dead inside. I understand that having kids isn't for everyone. But for me, the love I had for my son made me want to love myself more. It made me feel brand new. With Michael and Jude by my side, I had everything I never even knew I needed.

I used these feelings of love as a catalyst for change. I continued working on myself and began to transform into a confident woman little by little. I started taking risks and being a little more vulnerable and got a smidge braver bit by bit.

In 2011, we welcomed Ruby to our family. Having a daughter was a terrifying but adorable prospect for me. I didn't have confidence I could do a good job. I have always felt a disconnect with my ability to be close with other women because of the challenging relationship I had with my mom.

I realized over time that I needed to trust myself. I am not my mother, and growing up with an example of what NOT to do actually helped me be more sensitive and empathetic. I was given the opportunity to break the cycle of emotional and physical abuse in my lineage and be the person I wanted to be. I knew I needed to simply focus on trusting myself and my natural instincts. I recognized that if I wanted to be an example of confidence for my children, I had to actually feel it in my bones.

During my pregnancy with our last baby, Ozzy, I finally got to a breaking point where I cut off contact with my mother. I'd stopped returning my dad's letters from prison years back, but that's another story. It was heartbreaking to finally make the decision to end contact with them, but it was THE BEST GIFT I ever gave myself. Free from their abuse, narcissism, gaslighting, judgment, and toxicity, I became free and at peace in new ways.

I didn't realize how much I was still holding back who I was to make my family comfortable until I removed myself from the toxic environment. That's the thing about abuse—it's really hard to see how harmful it is until you remove yourself from it. I began wholly and unapologetically loving who I was and decided to use the pain of my past as jet fuel for my creative pursuits.

This not only benefited me on a personal level, but it blew my career wide open. Since ending contact with my family five-ish years ago, I have styled for BuzzFeed, blogged professionally, appeared on live TV, landed a killer job at a billion-dollar fashion company, won an award for my top-performing, self-produced podcast, and signed two book deals. I can't wait to see what I do next.

You can love someone and still know they do not deserve access to your life. You have to prioritize what is best for *your* emotional and mental health and make a commitment to yourself to stop apologizing for who you are and stop feeling shame about your imperfections.

If we want to reach our highest potential, we must learn to love ourselves without shame. I know it may seem scary to overcome whatever is holding you back from loving yourself, but not being boldly who you are is even scarier.

Bitch, Don't Kill My Vibe

Your mentality shapes your reality. When you stress out, things will stress out around you. Always control your thoughts and pacify any unnecessary stress. Control your vibrations and you are the master of your own harmony.

—Suzy Kassem, Rise Up and Salute the Sun

> **Energy** (*noun*) 1. The emotional output or vibes humans or environments give off 2. The amount of give-a-fuck required for completing mental, emotional, or physical tasks
>
> **Vibration** (*noun*) Our emotional tone, impact, atmosphere, state of being. The energy we give off to others around us

Think about the people you're most attracted to in your life. What do they have in common? For me, they are confident, funny, honest, loving, empathetic, and passionate. As emotional beings, we are naturally attracted to people who make us feel happy, safe, and energized.

The same can be said for attracting others to you. If your vibe is uninviting, insecure, ego-driven, or unsettled, it can cause others around you to feel stressed or robbed of their energy.

If you struggle to find your calm, use some of the tools suggested in this book (gratitude, meditation, journaling, mindfulness, etc.) for one month and see how they can transform your energy.

Your Body Is Bangin'

To me, beauty is about being comfortable in your own skin. It's about knowing and accepting who you are.
—*Ellen DeGeneres, comedian and talk show host*

> **Body image** (*noun*) The way we view our own body and how we feel about it

Not only is each body uniquely made, but attractiveness, like art, is completely subjective. Beauty is truly in the eye of the beholder, so why are we always trying to make our bodies look and feel like everyone else's?

Our body and mind make up our own unique vessel. We are individuals, not a generic copy of others. If you still can't find a way to celebrate yourself, try to find gratitude for what your body helps you accomplish each day. What has your body helped you achieve in life? Hopefully multiple orgasms, but it's also about the "little things," like helping us get to work, grow a human, or swim in the ocean. Think about all the things that your vessel has helped you experience and how you couldn't do most of them if you were just a brain in a jar.

Our body image can become so negatively influenced that we can be held back from reaching our goals or even working toward them at all. At one time, I was so self-conscious and ashamed of my appearance, I was afraid of strangers even seeing me. I would avoid eating in front of others or walking by groups of people because I was convinced they would start commenting about how fat, ugly, and disgusting I was.

One day, someone said to me, "Have you ever considered people are looking at you because they are thinking about how beautiful you are?" Um, no, actually I hadn't considered that for a second. Then I thought about all the times I looked at other people just to appreciate how beautiful or unique they were. This was a huge unlock for me about how mindset matters. It shifted my negative self-talk into a more compassionate view of myself and gave others around me the benefit of the doubt.

SOME EXAMPLES OF HOW NEGATIVE BODY IMAGE CAN HOLD US BACK

- Passing up a presentation or opportunity at work because we are afraid others will be judging how we look or talk
- Missing out on having fun with family or friends at the beach or pool because we don't want to be seen in a swimsuit
- Not traveling because we are afraid that we will take up too much space or will be judged by our size
- Missing out on memory making by avoiding having our photo taken
- Not applying for a job because we don't think we are attractive enough to work for a certain company

⚡ Avoiding new relationships because we fear rejection and shame

⚡ Not wanting to exercise outside or join a gym because we think people will judge us

⚡ Denying ourselves new clothing, vacations, or happiness until we can fit into a certain size or lose a certain amount of weight

⚡ Prioritizing diet culture (or other people's view of "health") over knowing our own body and what's right for ourselves

⚡ Setting a bad example for our children about what makes a person valuable or lovable

WAYS TO IMPROVE NEGATIVE BODY IMAGE

⚡ Work with a counselor to help dig into how your body image has been formed.

⚡ Avoid people, things, websites, TV shows, and social media accounts that make you feel like shit about your body.

⚡ Stop talking negatively about your weight and how you look to other people. This reinforces your own negative body image, and your insecure energy is contagious—it can be triggering and harmful to others.

⚡ Recognize and remind yourself that perfection doesn't exist—nor should it.

⚡ Don't judge other people by the way they look or choose to present themselves.

⚡ Talk to your body the way you'd want your child or loved one to talk to theirs.

⚡ Remember that the most interesting things about you have nothing to do with appearance.

Get All Up in Your Passions

Every great dream begins with a dreamer. Always remember, you have within you the strength, the patience, and the passion to reach for the stars to change the world.

—Harriet Tubman, American abolitionist and political activist

> **Passion** (*noun*) The stuff that makes us want to get out of bed on a rainy Sunday. A deep enthusiasm or love for something

Our passions help us survive all the mundane adulting we have to deal with on the daily. This craving to create (or whatever tickles your fancy) helps us connect with ourselves, others, and the universe at large.

We do not have to reserve our enthusiasm for things that make us money. Passion fuels our energy and happiness. Sure, in an ideal situation, you can make money from your passion but dollar bills aren't required to squeeze that sweet happiness juice out of the things you enjoy. I have been blessed (aka I've worked my ass off) to be able to turn multiple side projects into income and career building blocks, but it took years of work and portfolio expanding.

Making time for the things that make us feel obsession, enthusiasm, and fascination is a form of mental hygiene and self-care. Regardless of what we feel passionate about, when we prioritize our creative needs, we feel more satisfied with our lives. When your heart and soul get put into your work without considering the approval of others, you honor your unique vision and gift. That is where the magic is, all up in the you-est version of your work.

READY TO FEEL AWKWARD? GREAT.

What are your best qualities? Emotionally, physically, it all counts.

_____

_____

_____

_____

Has negative body image ever held you back from taking risks or trying something new? How can you overcome this in the future?

_____

_____

_____

_____

What are you most passionate about? What makes you feel the most calm, happy, and alive?

_____

_____

_____

_____

Finding Purpose

> "Carve your name on hearts, not tombstones.
> A legacy is etched into the minds of others
> and the stories they share about you."
>
> —*Shannon L. Alder, author*

> **Purpose** (*noun*) 1. The reason for which we exist 2. The motivation to reach a desired result 3. Grit, determination, resoluteness, tenacity

If I haven't drilled this down enough yet, one of my favorite mantras is *turn pain into purpose*. This personal mission statement of sorts has served me well so many times. Using this motto as a guiding principle has been very beneficial for me because it reminds me of my ultimate purpose: to use my experiences to help other people.

When I was considering launching my podcast *Something Was Wrong*, I was talking to my husband in the kitchen about the prospects of making the podcast, and I said, "What if everything I've overcome is for this reason?! What if this is my purpose?" He looked at me seriously and said sincerely, "Maybe it is." I knew he meant it and that he had faith in my abilities, but more importantly, I was able to say something so bold out loud to myself—and believe it.

My childhood and experiences blessed me with a deep connection to others' humanity, a high emotional IQ, a dark sense of humor, and empathic abilities. These have enabled me to work with other victims of emotional abuse and trauma and offer them empathy in a way I simply couldn't without my past.

This does not discredit the pain of my upbringing, but it does help me churn my adversity into helping others.

In 2012, my younger brother, Bobby, was murdered by a Los Angeles sheriff's deputy. It was the hardest, most painful thing I've ever experienced—seeing my baby brother whom I helped raise lying in a coffin at the age of 22.

The first year of grief was so consuming and rich in agony. However, I had two babies under the age of two at the time who needed their mama, and I wasn't about to let my pain stop me from being a great parent. It was extremely difficult and was made harder when Jude was diagnosed with autism spectrum disorder that year.

The year 2012 was one of the hardest ones for me to survive. I felt new lows I didn't think were possible. I decided this was probably a good time to get professional help for my anxiety and depression, so I made an appointment and started taking lifesaving medications that helped correct my brain's chemical imbalance.

Seeing someone lose their life needlessly at such a young age made me rethink my life and purpose. I didn't want to waste any more time or energy not living my truth and making the most of my opportunities. I needed to prioritize my mental health and path to healing.

I started my blog, *Lookie Boo*, during this shit year as a way to channel all these feelings and need for a creative distraction into my website. I let this awakening fuel my purpose to help other parents of kiddos with autism. I wanted to be open about my experience and celebrate all the amazing things autism brings into our lives. I didn't like the stigma that was attached to persons with special needs and chose to use my voice to fight it.

Being vulnerable and using my privilege helped me connect with other parents of kids with special needs, let me educate others, and gave me the therapeutic benefits of sharing my story and feeling validated.

I didn't have money to put into building my website, so I used passion instead. I built it from the ground up (with the help of a few awesome friends who know about computer stuff, thankfully). Though I had negative dollars in my bank account, I got creative with ways to start building. I leveraged free resources online, connected with local photographers (who were also looking to get the word out about their passions), and asked friends for help.

When I started building my blog, I was telling a "friend" about my excitement, and she said, "That seems like a lot of time to waste on something that won't make you money." Thankfully, I chose to ignore that negativity and believe in myself and my unique vision. Purpose has more value than money because you can't buy it.

Over time, I started to get contacted by brands, but they didn't want to pay me yet. I hadn't been "around long enough" for them to know my work, and I hadn't grown my audience to where it needed to be for paid work. So I began working with companies in exchange for product. They would send me clothes to showcase for free and I would work with a photographer to make sure the photos looked amazing and would make the brand excited. I focused on the bigger picture and future opportunities.

Thankfully, all of this time invested making zero dollars (for probably the first year) later led to me making a living from blogging. I gained so many incredible opportunities that came from passion alone. Eventually, I leveraged my success into working for brands, including a full-time "dream job" at a major fashion company in San Francisco. Really glad I didn't listen to that one hater who made me question investing time in myself and my passions.

The value didn't come from the work itself but from the happiness and joy of investing in what makes me feel most expressive. I could not have achieved the things I did without the pain that I suffered first—because it made me the strong woman I am today.

Whatever discomfort you have processed in your life, think of how you can use it to fuel your ambition and your unique vision.

Be Confident about Your Purpose

Listen, there's no such thing as being too confident in yourself. Confidence is simply offering yourself full trust in your powers and abilities. It empowers us to stand in our truth and own it.

Okay, I know that's way easier said than done, but with persistent hard work and prioritization, you can do anything.

Now, we can't sleep on that old bitch ego and her needy ass. Remember, confidence comes from working through hard shit, and ego comes from assuming you are the shit for no reason at all.

MORE WAYS TO BOOST CONFIDENCE

- Keep promises to yourself. When we do this, we build trust with ourselves and what we can accomplish.
- Affirm your vision and visualize your success. Daydreaming about where you want to go is one of the best ways to boost motivation. Do not hold back. Your limitation is what you decide it is.
- Take exquisite care of yourself. Self-care is an important way we show ourselves we are worthy of love and care. Don't let your life or passions overshadow your needs.
- Make lists and complete them. They don't have to be that deep—they can include simple things such as returning a text or making it to the grocery store.
- Invest in yourself—read a book (check!), take a class, go to that conference, ask someone to mentor you, whatever will help you achieve your goals.
- Write down the things you have already done that you are proud of.
- Ask others to describe you in one or two words, write them down, and put them somewhere you will see them each day.
- Spend time with other confident and happy people. Remember, those vibes are contagious, so who you hang with matters.

Just . . . GO!

The time to start is NOW. Well, not *now* now because you're going to (hopefully) finish this book first. But seriously, you should feel free to take a break and get your butt out there hustling the moment you're ready. You don't have to be perfect; you actually don't even need to know what you're doing! You are smart; you will figure things out as you go. Stop sitting on that idea and get to work. We learn and grow as we go. We are lucky to be living in a time when there is an endless amount of information, resources, and help out there to assist us.

When I started *Something Was Wrong*, I had absolutely— and I cannot stress this enough—no fucking clue what I was doing. I didn't know about podcast editing. But I didn't let that hold me back from trying. I trusted that I was smart and passionate enough to figure things out, and I was right. I had to start with the basics and build from there. YouTube and Google were my best friends and kinda still are. I am always evolving, but I know that each time I release an episode, I am putting every ounce of passion and purpose I have into it.

TAKE A PAUSE FOR PURPOSE

You're doing great, sweetie!

What do you consider your purpose? What fuels your passion?

_____

_____

_____

_____

What's an area in your life where you would like to feel more confident?

_____

_____

_____

_____

What motivates you to reach toward your goals?

_____

_____

_____

_____

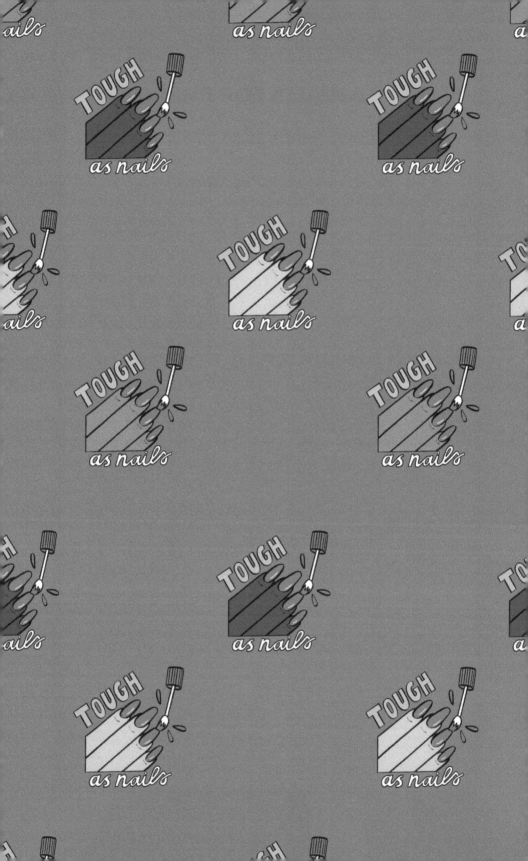

Give Yourself the Gift of Self-Compassion

(and Maybe Some Flowers)

> "Self-compassion involves treating yourself with the same kindness, concern, and support you'd show to a good friend. When faced with difficult life struggles, or confronting personal mistakes, failures, and inadequacies, self-compassion responds with kindness rather than harsh self-judgment, recognizing that imperfection is part of the shared human experience."
>
> —*Kristin Neff*, Self-Compassion:
> Stop Beating Yourself Up and Leave Insecurity Behind

Forgive (*verb*) 1. To stop resenting someone or something 2. To make peace with hard shit in order to free ourselves

Generous (*adjective*) The act or idea of being giving, charitable, considerate, big-hearted, hospitable, unselfish

Resentment (*noun*) The displeasure, sadness, or rage we feel toward an act, remark, or person who we feel has injured or harmed us

Self-compassion (*noun*) 1. Forgiveness or empathy toward ourselves 2. Accepting our imperfections with love

Part of what holds us back from stepping into our true potential is our inability to forgive ourselves for past *perceived* mistakes. We place so much importance on perfection, success (whatever we view that to be), and the opinions of others, we shame ourselves out of trying again.

When we look at the true definition of forgiveness, it's ultimately about letting go of past experiences that have caused you emotional injury or shame. Sometimes it's most difficult to forgive ourselves because we resent our insecurities and past *perceived* mistakes and stop trusting that we can make the right choices. If you have survived emotionally abusive relationships, it can be even harder to trust yourself.

This is why gratitude and generosity are so important for fighting shame and resentment. Gratitude reminds us of all the gifts we already hold; it highlights the opportunities we have had—not the outcomes. What if we gave ourselves the grace we gave to others? What could we accomplish if we generously, liberally, gifted forgiveness to past regrets and perceived failures? A shit ton.

Forgiveness Is Self-Care

Forgiveness isn't for the person who has hurt us. Forgiveness is for helping us move on—to cease resentment bubbling inside. So let us forgive with abandon, because ultimately we're the only people who suffer from a lack of forgiveness.

This act of compassion doesn't even have to be something that you discuss with the person you are harboring your resentment against. It can be a private conversation and decision you make within yourself. Light some sage, burn all your ex's photos, meditate, smash shit, journal it—whatever you need to do to let that poison evaporate. If we truly want to rise, we've got to let go of the things weighing us down.

Down Pillows Soften Screams Better Than Polyester Ones

In the Bible it says they asked Jesus how many times you should forgive, and he said 70 times 7. Well, I want you all to know that I'm keeping a chart.

—Hillary Clinton, politician, lawyer, and former First Lady

I hear ya, forgiveness is HARD AF—especially when we are trying to let go of the resentment and subsequent pain of those who have abused and harmed us (or those we love). Enjoying the process of forgiving someone is thankfully not a requirement, and it can take time, practice, and patience.

Sometimes it's a matter of finding how you can channel that pain and resentment on its way out. Maybe you like to scream into pillows, maybe you like to rage clean (same) or work it out at the gym—find whatever helps you release those resentments.

According to neuroanatomist Dr. Jill Bolte Taylor, our anger should only last for 90 seconds. NINETY. SECONDS. Just reading this made me pissed for 91 seconds. She asserts that if you have anger that lasts longer than 1.5 minutes, it's because you are replaying the story in your mind. Why is this harmful? Every time this happens, you trigger the response cycle all over again. Over time, reexperiencing these painful thoughts creates a negative physical response. This not only perpetuates negative self-talk and a fixed mindset, but the physical anxiety generates pain. This is another great reason for us to choose forgiveness and gratitude—they literally protect us from inflicting self-harm. I find that meditation and See's Candies truffles also help.

The Psychology of Positivity

Positive psychology is the "scientific study of human flourishing." Is that not the cutest thing ever—the science of happiness? People actually study all the factors that make it possible for people, organizations, and communities to thrive.

Dr. Martin E. P. Seligman, director of the University of Pennsylvania's Positive Psychology Center, asserts, "At the subjective level, the field of Positive Psychology is about valued subjective experience: well-being, contentment, and satisfaction (in the past); hope and optimism (for the future); and flow and happiness (in the present). At the individual level, it is about positive individual traits: the capacity for love and vocation, courage, interpersonal skill, aesthetic sensibility, perseverance, forgiveness, originality, future mindedness, spirituality, high talent, and wisdom."

So, like, WTF does *that* all mean? A great way to understand the concepts of positive psychology is to reference Dr. Seligman's **PERMA** model, which is made up of the five elements of well-being and positive thinking:

Positive emotion. Choose to think optimistically and observe our past, present, and future from a productive perspective.

Engagement. Engaging in our passions floods the brain with positive neurotransmitters and hormones that elevate our mood and overall well-being.

Relationships. We are hardwired for human connection and thrive when we have relationships that are built with love, intimacy, and healthy emotional and physical interaction.

Meaning. Discovering our individual purpose helps us find meaning and fulfillment in our lives. This can be through faith, career, family, artistic expression, sports—whatever makes you *you*.

Achievement. Having goals and accomplishments in life pushes us to thrive and flourish. This doesn't have to be winning an Olympic medal; it can be as simple as learning a new skill, taking a class, or walking a 5K.

If you are struggling with negative thinking, revisit this model and see if there is an area or two where you could be investing more time and energy. If you want to learn more, check out the list of Dr. Seligman's positive psychology books in the resources section at the end of this book.

Give the World the Gift of You

Shame research professor and goddess Dr. Brené Brown is my vulnerability guru. I've referenced her a few times in this book already. One of my favorite quotes of hers is "To create is to make something that has never existed before. There's nothing more vulnerable than that."

When we look at our individual creations and expressions of self as our art, there is truly nothing more personal. This is why discomfort and vulnerability are required elements of progress and authenticity—you must be unapologetically the most *you* version of *you* the universe has ever seen.

This brave act of being vulnerable, or exposed, honors who we are and celebrates others around us. So why does it feel so hard to be vulnerable sometimes? Shame, ego, perfectionism, and negative self-talk make exposing our authentic selves scary AF. We don't want to risk the possibility that a handful of people may not like us when there are so many others who love us for who we truly are.

Before I released the first season of *Something Was Wrong*, my husband sat me down and said, "A lot of people are going to love your podcast, and some people are going to hate it. I want you to prepare yourself for that now so you don't get upset if that happens." Of course my first recovering people-pleaser thought was "WAIT, WHO WON'T LIKE ME?! WHY?!"

I knew he was right, though. Not everyone is going to like you. They may even hate you or what your values and convictions are. It likely has nothing to do with you. At all. It's okay! Not everyone has to like us. One person not liking us does not make us less valuable. There are people who don't even like chocolate! When we are vulnerable and let others see our confidence and true selves, we not only allow for deeper connection, but we honor ourselves, our purpose, and our unique vision.

Sometimes we can be criticized and/or abused to the point that we stop trusting ourselves and our view of reality. A common coping mechanism is to start avoiding vulnerability at all costs to try to avert this shame. While hiding who we are might keep us from being criticized, it also keeps us from genuine connection.

As highlighted in the PERMA model, social interaction is an important piece of our positive well-being. According to Harvard

Women's Health Watch, "Dozens of studies have shown that people who have satisfying relationships with family, friends, and their community are happier, have fewer health problems, and live longer."

In her viral TED Talk, psychologist Susan Pinker argues, "Face-to-face contact releases a whole cascade of neurotransmitters and, like a vaccine, they protect you now, in the present, and well into the future, so simply shaking hands or giving somebody a high-five is enough to release oxytocin, which increases your level of trust, and it lowers your cortisol levels, so it lowers your stress." That's pretty amazing.

WE CAN WORK IT OUT

What is something you need to forgive yourself for?

_____

_____

_____

_____

_____

How can you show yourself more self-compassion?

_____

_____

_____

_____

_____

Who boosts your mood and makes you feel happy?

_____

_____

_____

_____

_____

BE PASSIONATE ABOUT YOURSELF

Your Brain Is a Liar ᴬᴺᴰ Its Pants Are on Fire

"How you love yourself is how you
teach others to love you"

—*Rupi Kaur*, Milk and Honey

Do you remember in English class when your teacher talked about the different types of narrators and how not all of them are trustworthy? We can often become our own unreliable narrators. In 1981, author William Riggan analyzed unreliable first-person narrators and grouped his findings into the following types:

The Pícaro. A narrator who is characterized by exaggeration and bragging; aka ego.

The Madman. A narrator who is experiencing only mental defense mechanisms, such as (posttraumatic) dissociation and self-alienation, or severe mental illness, such as schizophrenia or paranoia; aka mental health.

The Clown. A narrator who does not take narrations seriously and consciously plays with conventions, truth, and the reader's expectations; aka self-sabotage and procrastination.

The Naïf. A narrator whose perception is immature or limited through their point of view; aka our inner child.

The Liar. A mature narrator of sound cognition who deliberately misrepresents himself, often to obscure his unseemly or discreditable past conduct; aka impostor syndrome.

It's time to do some editing.

Let Your Subconscious In on Your New Reality

Remember our little frenemy, our subconscious hard drive where we store all of our experiences? Often, this pesky voice has been telling us some kind of false narrative about "who we are" for most of our lives. This is where a fixed mindset in our subconscious really takes hold of our progress. Thankfully, with a growth mindset, we can edit our story (and our unreliable narrators) anytime we damn please. It's not a drama—it's an EPIC choose your own adventure with a sense of humor, and you're the hero.

Show Your Ego Who's Really Boss and Get After It

Once we recognize our areas of opportunity, we are able to fill in the gaps and make adjustments to enable our success. Real change comes when we combine determination with a change in our routine and focus. Mind over matter is the use of willpower to overcome physical and emotional challenges. This is where "fake it 'til you make it" really comes in handy. You don't have to be free of impostor syndrome, negative self-talk, or any other productivity cockblockers in order to start pursuing your passions. You just have to start.

ROUTINE ROULETTE

We are creatures of habit, and the types of habits we perpetuate often influence our mental health. Having a routine is comforting to us because it allows us to foster habits that match our goals and aspirations.

COMMON SIDE EFFECTS OF NOT HAVING A ROUTINE

Stress. Not planning ahead and having a solid routine often causes more stress because we worry about when we will be able to "get it all done" without a plan of action.

Sleeplessness. Without creating and following a schedule, we risk constantly playing catch-up. Procrastination or anxiety over being able to complete needed tasks keeps us up at night, which furthers our exhaustion and the feeling of inadequacy.

Unhealthy coping mechanisms. Planning helps us avoid unhealthy habits such as poor eating, smoking, over-spending, lack of self-care, conflict, over-caffeinating, binge drinking, mindless scrolling/avoidance, self-harm, isolation, lack of physical activity, etc., etc.

What is your current weekly routine?

Monday _____

_____

_____

Tuesday _____

_____

_____

Wednesday _____

_____

_____

Thursday _____

_____

_____

Friday _____

_____

_____

Saturday _____

_____

_____

Sunday _____

_____

_____

Now, rewrite your routine, making time for passions, self-care, relationships, and reaching your goals. No pressure.

Monday_____

_____

_____

Tuesday_____

_____

_____

Wednesday_____

_____

_____

Thursday_____

_____

_____

Friday_____

_____

_____

Saturday_____

_____

_____

Sunday_____

Boom—you're ready to start your new routine. You may need to make adjustments through trial and error, but it's really that simple. Sure, we need to be flexible when changes arise that impact our routines, but having a plan and sticking to it benefits our mental health, promotes healthier habits, and gets us closer to those goals.

CHAPTER

10

Procrastination Is Perfection in Sheep's Clothing

> "A year from now you may wish you had started today."
>
> —*Karen Lamb, author*

> **Anxiety** (*noun*) 1. A feeling of uneasiness in our minds 2. Out-of-control, fear-driven doubt and negativity that distracts us
>
> **Fear** (*noun*) The (real or imagined) distressing emotion of dread, impending danger, compromised safety, looming threats of pain, injury, or death
>
> **Procrastination** (*noun*) 1. Avoiding important shit with very unimportant shit 2. Putting off starting a project or event that's important to us, usually because we are afraid of being imperfect

Ahhhhh, procrastination, everyone's favorite form of self-sabotage. Why do we do this to ourselves when we know it won't help? When I examined the motivations of why we procrastinate, I found that we are afraid to make a mistake. The idea of messing up something we care deeply about can make us freeze up, which is ironic because it often keeps us from progressing at all.

Maybe perfection isn't what's holding you back. Perhaps you're trying to evade vulnerability. You're just burnt out or feeling lazy. Whatever the cause, procrastination isn't helping.

Tell Perfectionism and Procrastination to Kick Rocks

Have you ever sat on a "big idea" or project that you hesitated acting on because you felt anxious or didn't know where to start? Me, too. It can take time and patience to let go of the fear and take the next step. It's overwhelming to make the leap sometimes, but you cannot have growth without discomfort. You won't find the time in your schedule; you must create the time yourself.

TIPS FOR AVOIDING PROCRASTINATION

- Create a schedule and stick to it.
- Set deadlines for yourself.
- Work in an area where you can avoid distractions and interruptions.
- Set reminders on your phone or write them where you'll see them daily.
- Ask someone to help hold you accountable. Actually let them hold you accountable.
- Take things a day at a time.
- Schedule breaks and commit to working in blocks of time.
- Start with the parts of your work that are giving you the most anxiety. It's rarely as difficult as we think it will be.

Fear Is a Time Suck

I have learned over the years that when one's mind is made up, this diminishes fear; knowing what must be done does away with fear.

—*Rosa Parks, civil rights activist*

I once heard that depression is the replaying of the past and anxiety is living in the future. Fear is a construct that boxes us into a fixed mindset about events that haven't even happened yet. Our attempt to predict the future and its outcomes is fruitless and exhausting. Anxiety and fear not only waste time and energy that can be invested in yourself or goals, they in no way help you actually predict the outcomes of life. You won't know until you start, so unless your goal is to become psychic, tell fear to suck it.

WAYS TO MAKE FEAR YOUR BITCH

Talk to someone about why fear is holding you back.
This can be a friend or mentor, though I highly recommend talking to a therapist or counselor if you're able. Make sure it's someone you trust and feel you will be able to be 100 percent honest with about what's holding you back.

Create an action plan. Getting started is scary for some—no shade! Make a list of small things you can do each day to move you closer to your goal. More on creating effective action plans to come.

Pump yourself TF up. Find a way to get hyped! I love making playlists and find that music really helps center me or get me going, depending on what I'm looking for.

Invest in yourself. If part of your hesitancy is that you feel you aren't knowledgeable enough to get started, begin by investing time educating yourself. This could be a class, book, degree, whatever you see fit.

Get Off That Beautiful Ass

Yes, relaxing is cool (like, *super cool*, TBH), but sometimes self-care can turn into . . . sloth care. Sometimes you just gotta push yourself to get your butt off that cushion you've spent so much time sitting on that you could make a ceramic casting of your ass. We've all been there.

We shouldn't use self-care as an excuse to avoid priorities. I often find myself in slumps like this after I haven't taken a day off work in far too long and I'm burnt TF out. Then I move into the other extreme: complete inaction. I'm still trying to find the right work-life balance, and really, that's all we can do—keep trying.

TIPS FOR FINDING BALANCE BETWEEN OVERWORKING YOURSELF AND SLOTH CARE

⚡ Make time in your schedule/routine for work and play.

⚡ Reward yourself for accomplishing your to-do list with an act of self-care.

⚡ Say no to things that are not essential—overbooking yourself because you don't want to say no to things/people is not selfless, it's stupid.

⚡ If your mental health holds you back from caring for yourself properly, consider making a daily self-care checklist to hold yourself accountable. You deserve time to take a shower and wash your ass just like everyone else.

⚡ Include healthy habits in your self-care routine, such as going for a walk, meditating, spending time with a friend, getting extra sleep, practicing affirmations, journaling, taking a bath, etc.

⚡ Carve out a day of the week when you avoid making any unnecessary plans. For me, this is Sunday. Sure, things do come up from time to time, but most often my family and I commit to spending time together on Sundays.

Passion Is the Antidote to Procrastination

Here's the thing: Anyone can make plans to pursue their dreams or side hustle, but without passion, it's extremely hard to find the motivation to complete what's necessary to propel you forward. Passion is the not-so-secret ingredient that is an absolute must—and if you've purchased this book, I'm confident you have many passions worth pursuing in your life.

When I was editing the first season of *Something Was Wrong*, I was working 40 hours a week at my day job and keeping my three kids alive. I had to sacrifice months and months' worth of weekends (normally my only downtime) to work on the podcast. I knew I had no idea what I was doing, so I needed to over-estimate how long the process would take. I had to give myself permission to take the time and space that I needed to succeed. Before I began working on weekends, I sat down with my hus-band and told him my goals and what kind of support I would need from him in order to reach them. Thankfully, he encouraged me and took on solo parenting and various other household tasks during these times so that I could focus intently. Most valiantly, he took the kids to children's birthday parties without me. Not all heroes wear capes.

Let's be real, though: Do I want to work weekends for the rest of my life? Hell no. It's a season of struggle for the greater hustle. Sometimes you just have to put your head down and get to work. Create a realistic plan, schedule the time, stay on task when the time comes, and use every minute productively. You can scroll Instagram while you take a dump later. I promise Susan's new haircut can wait.

OKAY, BUT, LIKE, WHAT IF *I DON'T KNOW* WHAT I'M PASSIONATE ABOUT?

For some, passions don't come "naturally," or perhaps you have so many that it feels difficult to narrow them down. Thankfully, recent research out of Stanford University suggests that passions can be developed. Researchers examined whether interests were fixed qualities that are naturally occurring or just waiting to be discovered. The good news is that both things seem to be true. For some, passion seems to come effortlessly, while others may need to take time, a growth mindset, and education to fully develop their passions. No matter how natural or "developed" your passion feels, it doesn't determine the outcome; only your hard work does that.

IDENTIFY BARRIERS AND THEN BURN THEM DOWN

We have discussed a lot of hurdles that keep us from taking the leap. Now it's time to be honest and write them down.

What has previously held you back from acting on your passion or goals?

_____

_____

_____

_____

_____

_____

How are you going to burn these barriers to the ground and get after it?

_____

_____

_____

_____

_____

_____

What are two things you are going to do THIS WEEK to move you closer to your goal(s)?

(Examples: Send that email, write that proposal, ask for a raise, ask someone to mentor you, start your action plan, etc.)

1. _____

_____

_____

_____

2. _____

_____

_____

_____

The way I'm going to complete these two actions is:

_____

_____

_____

_____

_____

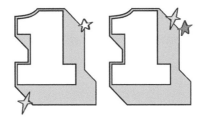

This Is the Sign You've Been Looking For

> "Your inner voice is your signboard, follow it."
>
> *—Anamika Mishra, author and motivational speaker*

Habit (*noun*) A pattern of choice we make consciously and subconsciously in our lives

Sign (*noun*) 1. Any person, place, thing, action, event, or pattern we interpret to have meaning other than what is originally intended 2. An indication, clue, or token from our life that we feel conveys a meaning

If we sit idly by waiting for some magic sign from the universe that we are supposed to begin working toward our goals, we will be wasting a lot of time. Instead, we can listen to our inner voice and actually move toward our accomplishments.

Often, before we've even begun the work, our minds like to create wild, anxiety-inducing, soap-opera-like outcomes of our worst fears. Or our ego creates massive expectations that are completely unrealistic and set us up for perceived failure. We put too much pressure on ourselves.

Ultimately, the work begins when we decide it does. Today can be the first day of our adventure and the last day of bad habits. We control the path we take and when and how we choose to begin and end our efforts.

Embrace self-love and compassion, make a freaking plan, and let's get this shit done.

Fake It 'Til You Rake It (Up)

I do a weird thing when I am nervous where I tilt my head back like I am super confident. This is my attempt to fake it until I make it, or at the very least make it easier for someone to slit my throat.

—Amy Poehler, Yes Please

> **Fake it 'til you make it** (*aphorism*) An English saying that implies if we imitate competence, confidence, and an optimistic growth mindset, we can accomplish our desired results with time, experience, and practice

Nobody wakes up one day and suddenly has the ability to create art, music, photos, podcasts, films, or writing—they just do it. Authenticity is one of the most important things in the world to me, but sometimes you just gotta fake it until you make it. I personally think of this mantra more like *faith it 'til you make it*. It's not acting disingenuous or being inauthentic; it's having the faith that if we simply try, we will figure it out eventually. This doesn't make you an impostor; it makes you a work in progress.

If you are struggling to trust your abilities, *observe* these feelings instead of allowing your emotions to overcome you. Ask yourself: Why am I feeling this way? What's making me believe I can't do this? What are the facts? What is something else challenging I've accomplished? You will find that by observing what is the truth versus what is your perceived truth, you can shift your perspective.

WAYS TO CONVINCE YOURSELF THAT YOU KINDA KNOW WTF YOU'RE DOING

Study the work of people who have done this before. Take inspiration from the successes and areas of opportunity of those who have already accomplished what you dream of. Don't forget to make sure your art reflects your unique perspective.

Practice until you pass out. Get really comfortable with the things that scare you most about pursuing your passions. Once you've knocked down your biggest barriers, you know you can handle anything.

Find your people. Connect with others who are already working in the industry of your enthusiasm. Learn from the mistakes of others. You may need to pay for consulting, but often the wisdom and insights you gain save you money and time in the long run.

Educate yo' self. There isn't much in life as valuable as good old-fashioned knowledge. Read all the books, listen to all the podcasts, google everything, and watch all the YouTube tutorials. Become an expert of your craft. The more you know, the more you grow.

Visualize your success. Try closing your eyes and visualizing positive outcomes. Let's say you want to learn to do a cartwheel. Replaying the times you've tried and failed will not enable you to feel confident in your ability to flip your shit. However, if you close your eyes and envision yourself completing the cartwheel, you shift your energy and open your mind to positive results. It's a simple change that has a big impact when we are chasing our dreams. Mind over matter, well, matters.

Take extra care of your extra ass. Prioritizing your personal and mental hygiene is highly important for sustaining or improving your state of mind. Make time for exercise, those you love, and rest.

Ghost Garbage Habits for Good

According to author Robert Taibbi, an expert in cognitive behavioral therapy, breaking bad habits is not about stopping but about substituting. So instead of thinking of how we should stop doing something, we actually just need to find a positive behavior to replace it.

HOW TO REPLACE BAD HABITS

1. **Define the concrete behavior you want to change or develop.** Write down a specific habit that you want to replace in your routine.

2. **Identify the triggers.** Reflect on what influences you to make certain choices. Thinking ahead helps us cope in advance.

3. **Ditch the triggers.** Eliminate and avoid triggers in your environment as much as possible.

4. **Develop a substitute plan.** Prepare a replacement for your habit. For example, if you bite your nails when you are feeling anxious, try carrying a stress ball, gum, or something else you can use to release that restless energy.

5. **Change the larger pattern.** Evaluate your routine and daily choices from a bird's-eye view. By examining the larger patterns of your behavior, you make it easier to tackle the core habit. Also, this helps you exercise your willpower on smaller, easier pattern-breaking behaviors. This can add to your sense of empowerment.

6. **Use prompts.** Thoughtfulness and awareness help set us up for success. Use physical reminders and/or reminders on your calendar/phone.

7. **Get support.** Find an accountability buddy who can enable your success by encouragement or knowledge of breaking such a habit.

8. **Support and reward yourself.** Reward yourself when you meet smaller goals within your larger ambitions. For example, if your bad habit is spending money on coffee drive-thrus, reward yourself after two weeks with a pedicure or some other kind of self-care.

9. **Be persistent and patient.** Take each day at a time. Mistakes will happen; give yourself grace.

10. **Consider getting professional help.** If you're still feeling overwhelmed or in need of extra support, consider talking to a counselor or attending a topical support group.

COMMIT TO BREAKING THE HABIT

What bad habit(s) do you want
to eliminate?

_____

_____

_____

_____

What habits can you substitute for
these behaviors?

_____

_____

_____

_____

How will you hold yourself accountable?

_____

_____

_____

_____

Awww shiiiiiiit, we made it to part 3! Now that we've discussed the lame things that keep us from reaching our highest selves, it's time to do the damn thing. Because internalizing our victories is important, let's celebrate the work you've begun on yourself. Go you!

When pursuing my passions, I've had to invest a lot of time and energy up front. I've had to find time in my schedule that wasn't already committed to all my other responsibilities and make the most of it. I created goals, set timelines, and held myself accountable.

Once I got over the anxiety and fear of making a mistake or thinking about how hard things were going to be, I was able to let go and enjoy the process. I decided that even if no one else cared about the art I conceived, knowing I accomplished what I set my mind to would be enough. I knew I would never regret keeping that promise to myself.

Honestly, I think that's when you know you are working where you are "meant to be": when you hope for the best outcome but enjoy the adventure so much you find inner success no matter what. I was at a really low point in my life when I decided to make some changes and start pursuing podcasting. The journey of creating goals, keeping promises to myself, working with others, and seeing the end product was extremely therapeutic and confidence-boosting for me.

We can dream and fantasize, or we can hustle and see dreams realized. The choice is up to us. Crack those knuckles and get hydrated, bitches—it's go time.

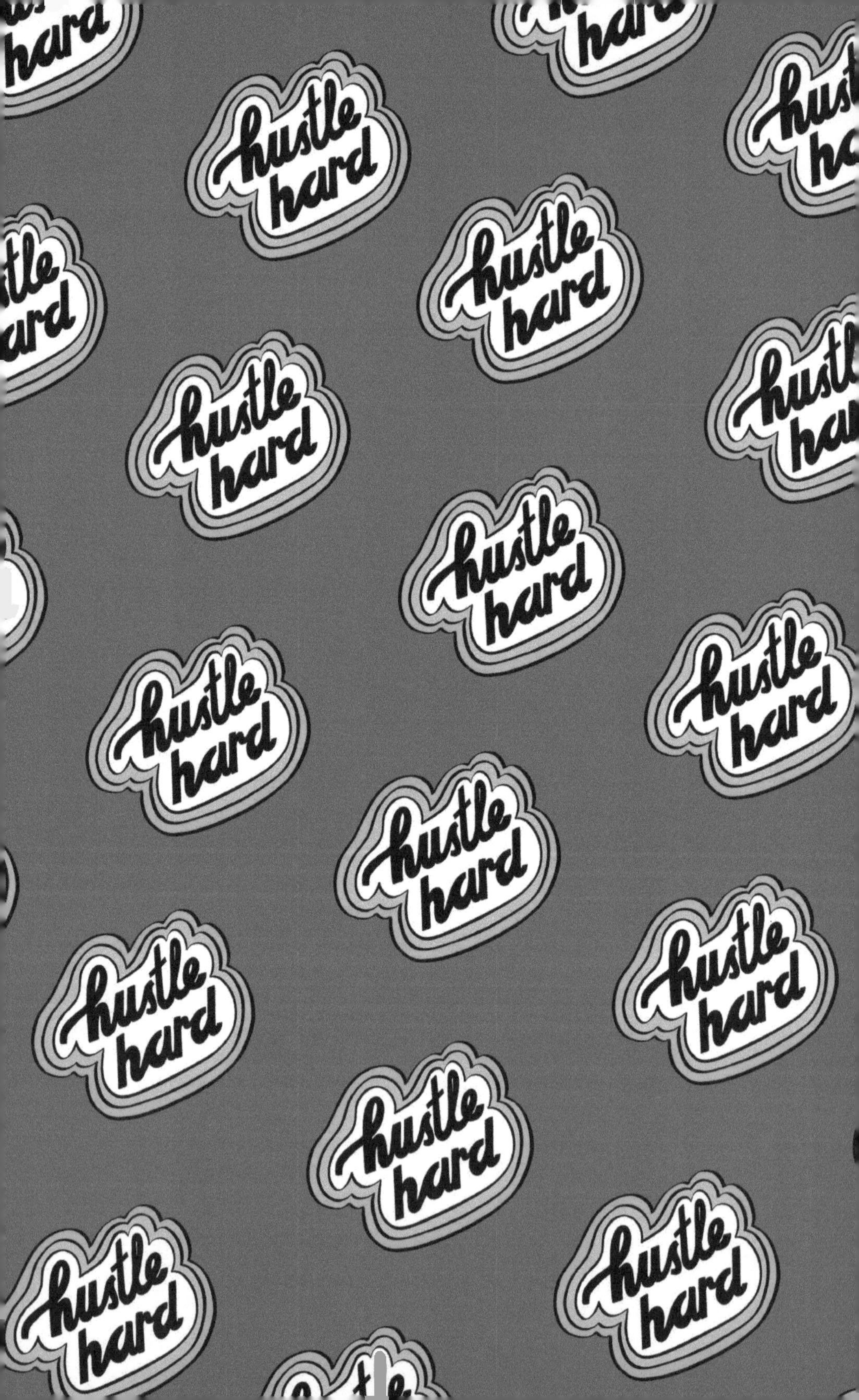
hustle hard

Commit to Failing Faster

> "You may encounter many defeats, but you must not be defeated. In fact, it may be necessary to encounter the defeats, so you can know who you are, what you can rise from, how you can still come out of it."
>
> —*Maya Angelou, poet, memoirist, and civil rights activist*

> **Commit** (*verb*) Promise to execute an action
>
> **Failure** (*noun*) An outcome we regard as unsuccessful, lacking purpose or growth
>
> **Success** (*noun*) 1. The desired outcome of attempted endeavors 2. Accomplishing our intended goals

In the age of social media, it's easy to imagine that people's success magically appears one day the same way it pops up on your feed. What we don't see on the highlight reels of those we admire is the sweat, sacrifice, swearing, sobbing, and sucking that come first.

We can choose courage, or we can choose comfort. Achievement is reached through persistent hard work, which often includes failing first. The opposite of success is not failure; it's giving up.

Create SMART Goals

You're anything but basic, and your goals shouldn't be, either.

> **SMART goals** (*noun*) SMART is an acronym that stands for **S**pecific, **M**easurable, **A**chievable, **R**elevant, and **T**imely. A SMART goal incorporates all of these criteria to help focus your efforts and increase the chances of achieving that goal.

Using the SMART goal method helps ensure that we're checking for blind spots, creating practical goals, and setting ourselves up for success.

HOW TO CREATE A SMART GOAL

Be specific. Clarity of your goals is essential. What do you want to accomplish? Why is this goal important? Who is involved? What resources or support will you require?

Make it measurable. Tracking progress is not only motivating, but it helps us anticipate our future needs to continue meeting this and new goals. Instead of saying, "My goal is to meditate more," you'd say, "My goal this week is to meditate three times." At the end of the week, you know exactly how to assess whether this goal was met.

Ensure it's achievable. Our goals should push our abilities but still remain possible. Break down your larger vision into smaller digestible and achievable tasks. If your ambitions require funding, for example, create a budget before you begin.

Confirm relevancy. This step is about establishing goals that matter to *you* and making sure that they align with your greater purpose. When in doubt, ask yourself, *Does this support the work?* If the answer is no, don't waste time on it.

Make it timebound. Use short-term goals to help build long-term success. What do you want and need to achieve today, this week, this month? If we don't keep ourselves on schedule, no one else will.

Be Strong Enough to Suck at Something New

We're all risk-averse creatures, aren't we? Like turtles, hiding in our little shells, trying to protect ourselves—never quite realizing that we're protecting ourselves from the good stuff as well as the bad.

—Debbie Johnson, author and poet

> **Change** (*noun*) The feeling or description of something new, fresh, and/or developing. Something different than its original form
>
> **Discomfort** (*noun*) A lack of comfort. For example, the way I feel when I have to take a dump in a public restroom

Stepping out of our comfort zones is freeing but also nap-inducing. Fear of the unknown can be intimidating but is necessary for positive change. How many incredible things have happened in your life because you accepted change or tried new things?

No matter what you are working toward, it's important to keep an open mind focused on progress, not perfection. Start by celebrating change—viewing newness as goodness. Real development comes from staying flexible and continuing to be resilient.

Be an Unapologetic Beginner

Have you ever felt annoyed, embarrassed, or defeated because you didn't master a task or skill at first try? Guilty. These negative feelings come from shame, frustration, entitlement, and/or ego. Why is it that we expect ourselves to know how to do something WE HAVE LITERALLY NEVER DONE BEFORE? Expectations matter.

By leveraging a growth mindset and using the SMART goal method, you can create an action plan that is built to scale all your current knowledge and experience. As you spend time improving your craft, your goals will naturally evolve as you do. Hell yeah.

Get In on the Action

> **Action plan** (*noun*) A detailed outline of the actions needed to reach a goal

Action plans help us create a proposed strategy of steps and/or tasks that move us closer to our goals. Think of your action plan as a map guiding you along this adventure. It helps you plan for the future, set yourself up for success, and predict possible challenges.

HOW TO DRAFT AN AWESOME ACTION PLAN

Draft SMART goals. Use the SMART method we discussed earlier when drafting your objectives.

Create milestones. Within your larger ambitions, create check-in milestones. These can be timebound or workbound.

Plan action lists. Under each SMART goal, create a list of tasks that you need to complete.

Give yourself due dates. Establish deadlines and stick to them. You are your own boss; be a hard-ass.

Ruthlessly prioritize. Be thoughtful about which order your tasks should go in.

Determine needed resources and materials. Identify what tools, supplies, resources, materials, programs, and equipment you will need. If you need to create a plan for how you will acquire these things, make a list.

Prepare a budget. You may need to invest in equipment or resources to aid your achievements, so drafting a budget is an important part of identifying realistic SMART goals.

Schedule your time. Creating lists and plans is fruit-less without follow-through. Life is busy, so you have to schedule the time in your day/week for executing this plan. The time doesn't just appear; you create it. I'm also a big believer in rest. So don't forget to take time off to rest your mind and replenish energy as well.

Check in on yourself. An action plan is pointless unless you actually use it. Calendar specific times each day/week to track and evaluate your progress.

THINK SMART

It's time to practice drafting your own SMART goal. This should be an actual goal you will work toward this week/month/year.

Specific: What is your clear-cut goal? Be as precise as possible.

_____

_____

_____

_____

Measurable: How will you gauge whether this goal has been met?

_____

_____

_____

_____

Achievable: Is there anything that will keep you from meeting this benchmark? What challenges do you anticipate?

_____

_____

_____

_____

Relevant: How does this milestone support your greater vision?

_____

_____

_____

_____

Timebound: When will you complete this goal? Be as specific as possible.

_____

_____

_____

_____

Prioritize: This Shit Is Urgent!

One of the things I realized is that if you do not take control over your time and your life, other people will gobble it up. If you don't prioritize yourself, you constantly start falling lower and lower on your list, your kids fall lower and lower on your list.

—Michelle Obama, lawyer, author, producer, and former First Lady

> **Prioritize** (*verb*) Determine what is most timely and important

Okay, *some* of this shit is urgent. Other stuff isn't a good use of our time. And with time being such a nonrenewable resource, we should probs be careful with how we spend it. Prioritizing is ultimately about time management. You have the same number of hours in a day as Beyoncé—use them well. I mean, most of us don't have the same resources as Beyoncé, but sometimes you gotta think big.

HOW TO PRIORITIZE LIKE A LEADER

- Create and stick to your action plan. Look at you, all fancy with an action plan.
- Sort your to-do list by due dates.
- Work on your most challenging projects early in the day when you're freshest.
- Say no to things that don't serve your work/goals. Making time for family is one thing; saying no to Suzy's new book club is another. Before you make commitments, consider how they impact your dreams.

- Get off your phone and social media. Schedule breaks where you allow yourself to mindlessly scroll for a specific amount of time.
- Use timers, alarms, clocks, calendars, WHATEVER to help you keep track of time. I use my iPhone alarms so I don't have to worry about looking at my phone to check the time.

Become a Balance Brainiac

Don't get so busy making a living that you forget to make a life.
—Dolly Parton, singer

> **Balance** (*noun*) Equality or equivalence in weight, parts, schedule, or emotion

Finding the right balance between work, passions, play, family, friends, and rest is an ongoing process. Without striking the right harmony, we can find ourselves feeling burnt out and/or discouraged.

Finding the right mix of life may take several attempts, and then life shifts and you start all over again. Flexibility aids balance and helps us manage expectations.

Make sure to include time in your schedule for human connection and rest. We often think we don't need these things or sacrifice them because we don't view them as essential. Isolation, overcommitment, and burnout will catch up to us if we don't prioritize balance.

EVERY SETBACK IS A SETUP FOR A COMEBACK

Success requires passion, determination, and resilience. We will make mistakes. We will get knocked down. We must leverage our pain and adversity into passion-fueled purpose. If all else fails, learn to laugh at yourself and not take yourself too seriously.

Reaching your goals requires ongoing commitment to flexibility, self-compassion, and—you guessed it—a growth mindset. You've got this. And even if you don't, you'll get this.

How can you better manage your time?

_____

_____

_____

What are your highest priorities at the moment?

_____

_____

_____

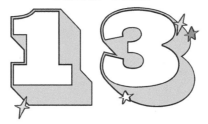

Put Money in Context: It's a Tool, Not an Identity

> "Don't think money does everything or you are going to end up doing everything for money."
>
> —Voltaire, writer and philosopher

> **Abundance** (*noun*) Having more than enough of a feeling, object, wealth, or attitude
>
> **Money mindset** (*noun*) 1. The attitude with which you think about your finances and financial capabilities 2. The influence you have in making key financial decisions
>
> **Scarcity** (*noun*) Short or dwindling supply of something. Insufficiency or infrequency
>
> **Wealth** (*noun*) 1. A surplus of money or valuable shit 2. An abundance of anything

If you are looking to measure your success by monetary compensation alone, you will likely never find satisfaction. Sure, money is great and helps us stay alive, but it's not everything.

When I began blogging (in the pre-influencer and VSCO girl era), I didn't make any money at all the first year. I thankfully had very minimal costs (because we were living paycheck to paycheck), so the main resource being put into my work was my time. I was in the dishwashing stage of my hustle, and I wasn't going to turn down any brand partnerships, even if they only offered me free stuff and not money.

Once my audience grew and I knew what I was offering was quality, unique content, I was able to price my rates accordingly with paid contracts.

After making it to that point, I didn't take unpaid work anymore. It's important to have self-awareness about not only the quality and value of your work but the industry standards for how rates or costs are determined. Bottom line: Don't be shortsighted when you are starting out. Sometimes you have to work for free to get to the larger fee.

Every single creative income source I've built has evolved from tiny budgets. I didn't have the money to buy a fancy camera and Photoshop when I started my fashion blog. I trusted that my styling vision would be unique and strong enough to stand on its own. Thankfully, I was right. There are seasons to the hustle—enjoy each one.

Start with What You Do Have (Abundance Is Awesome!)

In chapter 5, we talked about having an abundance mindset— believing there's enough wealth, prestige, and happiness to go around. This includes you! It can feel so disheartening when you are broke and struggling to meet your needs. I get it. I've slept in my car. I've visited food banks. It's terrifying and can feel debilitating. In those moments it's difficult to see a way out. Once I did get back on my feet, it sure as hell made me appreciate what I had so much more.

Don't get me wrong; there is nothing wrong with money. I'd love to swim in a mansion of money like Scrooge McDuck. But it's when we fail to recognize our actual wealth versus our perceived wealth that we sell ourselves short. For example, you might have less money than Lady Gaga, but what if you compared what you have to someone living well below the poverty line? Context matters.

If you are scared to pursue your passions because of your own scarcity (aka your bank account is negative—been there), think about the abundance you do have. This can be grit, heart, talent, or passion. Ultimately, these types of wealth offer the most value when manifesting our vision.

EXAMPLES OF ABUNDANCE

- Love
- Health
- Happiness
- Peace
- Confidence
- Money
- Intelligence
- Emotional intelligence
- Freedom

Make Over Your Money Mindset

In order to transform our mindset from scarcity to abundance, we must recognize our unhealthy financial habits that could be holding us back from flourishing.

IDEAS FOR IMPROVING YOUR MONEY MINDSET

Make a plan. Creating a budget enables us to plan ahead, anticipate needs, and avoid overspending.

Stop emotionally spending. Instead of looking to new objects to bring you joy, find happiness in a self-care activity such as taking a bath, spending time with a friend, or creating something with your hands.

Don't compare. Other people's finances are none of our business, and vice versa. With an abundance mentality, we know that the wealth of others in no way robs us of our own opportunities.

Start small. If you do struggle with saving or staying within your budget, consider starting small, like saving $1 a week. Not only will you stash a li'l cash, but you will also practice self-control and keeping promises to yourself.

Your Vision Isn't Worth a Check

While blogging professionally, I got lots of emails and offers for brand partnerships that just didn't feel right for me and my audience or align with my values. At first, it was really hard for me to turn down these opportunities, mostly because we were broke. Nevertheless, I knew I didn't want to jeopardize who I was and what I believed in for a few hundred bucks. The cost of the loss of your reputation or others' trust in you is not worth it. Don't be shortsighted. If you're truly developing your passion for the long haul, commit to staying authentic to yourself.

Abundance Is Gold.
Let's Get to Mining.

According to spiritual wellness guru Deepak Chopra, there are various ways you can practice exercises for creating abundance. Two examples of ways to practice recognizing abundance:

1. **Self-image:** At the start of your day, think of a particular color to bring into your life. Throughout your day, pay close attention to the plethora of ways the universe shows you this shade. At the end of the day, journal your experience. What, if anything, surprised you? What trends did you see?

2. **Monetary:** Visualization is a powerful technique for generating abundance, especially if you are a "visual person."

Physical reminders can help motivate and remind you of your goals. As a young, broke actor, Jim Carrey wrote himself a check for $10 million for "acting services rendered." He kept the check in his wallet for five years until he found out he was going to make $10 million on his movie *Dumb and Dumber*. Try this exercise by writing yourself a check. Include specific and measurable ways you are going to earn this payment. Let go of limiting or negative thoughts. Place this visual somewhere you can see it each day.

HAVE A HEART-TO-HEART WITH CASH

Once you know just how much money you'll need to accomplish your dream, there's a good chance you'll feel less stressed about it. Infinity is much more intimidating than hard numbers, so take the time to plan instead of letting your imagination wander.

How confident do you feel in your money mindset? What are your areas of opportunity?

_____

_____

_____

What does abundance mean to you?

_____

_____

_____

Do you need funds to reach your goal? If so, how do you plan to earn or save for these resources?

_____

_____

_____

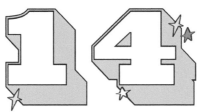

Actions Walk, Words . . . Well, Talk

> "I hope my actions speak more for me
> in the future than my hashtags!"
>
> —Louise Linton, actor

> **Cheap talk** (*noun*) Communication between players
> (often in video games) that does not directly affect the
> payoffs of the game. Conversation (usually shallow)
> that doesn't concern the real subject or purpose of the
> conversation
>
> **Hater** (*noun*) A person who greatly dislikes a specified
> person or thing. A negative or critical person that is probs
> just projecting their insecurity or scarcity/fixed mindset
> on others
>
> **Internet troll** (*noun*) Bored AF dicks who pick fights
> online or say wild shit to get the attention or approval
> of other people online. Cowards who harass, criticize,
> bully, antagonize, or lie about others as a way to distract
> themselves from their self-hatred

We can talk about our goals until we pass out, but unless we take action toward said goals, it's pretty fucking pointless, TBH. I've had people ask me how I find the time to get things done. The truth is I don't—I make it. I've had others ask me how I got started podcasting. Honestly, I just started. There isn't some magical elf waiting in the forest with a "now's the time" bell that's going to come out and summon you. You either do it or you don't.

We are human, things come up, and changing and staying flexible is important. Some days, life simply takes over, and despite your best efforts, you just can't get done that day what you had planned. This is very different from making time to do something and waking up and deciding you "just don't feel like it." Feelings should not always dictate our actions. Sometimes you really do have to suck it up and just get back to work. Again, it's not about perfection but about progress. Our actions are an expression of our personal priorities.

The cheap talk of others is also meaningless without action to back up their opinions. I read an (anonymous) quote last night that said, "Stop asking blind people to proofread your vision," and it's so true. It's so important to protect your vision and ignore the input of people who haven't done the work before.

Ignore Haters and Trolls

As you start crushing those goals, you may encounter some haters and trolls. This is especially true if you plan to share your art and/ or accomplishments online. As a recovering people-pleaser, this has been a growth opportunity for me. While I have very strong creative abilities and a confident vision, I tend to doubt myself when others do.

When those negative podcast reviews started to roll in, I got so distracted from my work and caught up in the emotions. I wasted so much time concerned about the feedback of random people with horrible screen names. I started doubting myself, my art, and my vision. Thankfully, with the encouragement of my loved ones and a few TED talks, I was able to realize that trying to please everyone doesn't work. In attempting to do so, we only cloud our viewpoint and deplete our energy—the very things we need to be successful. I do my best to avoid negativity as much as possible. This doesn't mean I'm not interested in improving my craft or growing; it just means I'm selective about whom I trust to help me do so.

You Can't Make Everyone Love You (Trust Me, I've Tried)

When you're different, sometimes you don't see the millions of people who accept you for what you are. All you notice is the person who doesn't.

—Jodi Picoult, Change of Heart

In my experience, the best way to deal with haters and trolls is to separate yourself and ignore them as much as possible. Your vision is too strong and your to-do list too long to waste time on the opinions of the people who don't get you. When we honor who we are over the opinions of others, we stay aligned with our vision and attract those who resonate with our art.

Social Media Is That Jerk You Dated Again, and Again, and Again

Ugh, social media, where people will literally judge and fight about anything.

Between Pinterest birthday parties and pink-filtered Instagram models in thongs, it's no wonder social media is a breeding ground for narcissism and insecurity. Just thinking about the comments section on Facebook and YouTube gives me crotch-sweats.

Don't get me wrong, I love and need the Internet, but it totally sucks sometimes. Social media is great for staying connected with friends and family, gaining inspiration, and networking. The Internet is required at most schools and jobs nowadays. So how can we scroll the Web without letting it mess with our head?

HOW TO INTERNET LIKE A BOSS

- Unfollow any account that makes you feel like shit.
- Don't argue with strangers—or anyone else if you can avoid it.
- Don't feed the trolls.
- Limit the time you spend online.
- Block all frenemies and sociopaths.
- Share what feels right for you.
- Encourage others—cheer on a friend with a supportive comment or message.
- Be authentic and loyal to your IRL values.
- Use your privilege and voice to help the silenced.
- Stand up for what you believe in.
- Remember that social media is a highlight reel.
- Do not waste your valuable time lurking on your ex or the people who have hurt you.
- Follow accounts that make you feel warm and fuzzy. For me, that's babies, puppies, and baby pigs.
- Give others the benefit of the doubt.
- Reserve your judgment on subjects that hurt no one.
- Speak your truth in kindness.

Be Selective with Your Squad

I have learned who my "real friends" are during the lowest and highest parts of my life. It's important to filter the comments you allow into your life online, but it's way more important when it comes to your friends IRL. As you blossom into your highest self, you may be surprised to notice some people aren't too happy to see you doing well. This likely has to do with their own journey or thinking with a scarcity mindset.

My friends Sara and Alissa (who were subjects on the first season of *Something Was Wrong*) were the most encouraging, supportive, and helpful friends a person could hope for. Having them cheer me on and remind me when I was freaking out about stupid shit was invaluable to me. When I doubted myself, they said, "Girl, you got this." When something awesome happened, they celebrated me. I am forever grateful. If you are lucky to have Saras and Alissas in your lives, remember to return the favor when it's their time to shine.

GO DO SOMETHING COOL

Since we focused on the power of actions in this chapter, instead of asking you to write something down, I'm going to encourage you to instead take five minutes to complete something you have been putting off. It's amazing how much you can accomplish in five minutes when you are intently focused on the task at hand.

How Hard Do You Love Yourself Right Now?

> "You can't be that kid standing at the top of the waterslide, overthinking it. You have to go down the chute."
>
> —Tina Fey, comedian and writer

Self-love (*noun*) The love we have for ourselves

Narcissism (*noun*) 1. The belief that one's needs, feelings, ideas, or beliefs are more important than those of others. Selfishness 2. Excessive infatuation with oneself

Just as there is a great distinction between confidence and ego, there is a massive difference between loving yourself and narcissism. Narcissism is shallow and selfish. Conversely, self-love is kind and supportive.

When working as a stylist for a major fashion brand, something that came up a lot in conversations with my female coworkers was how much we felt we were raised to look down on speaking highly of ourselves and our accomplishments. The general consensus seemed to be that we were made to feel we should never come across as prideful or braggy. It's not that I don't think men don't struggle with self-image; it's that society hasn't historically tried to silence their equality since the beginning of time. Who benefits from women feeling inferior and being silenced about their success? It's not women.

I have a daughter who I am raising to recognize her accomplishments, and I truly believe the best way to teach her this is living by example. Instead of focusing my compliments on the way she looks, I highlight her intelligence, bravery, vulnerability, growth, determination, kindness, etc. She's listening to the way I talk to her and how I talk to myself. This is why I'm extra careful to talk to myself in a way I would want my daughter to talk to herself.

Be your own soulmate and the president of your fan club.

Let Your Support System Love You, Too

As a fiercely independent Aries, I find asking for the help of others (outside my immediate family) to be a struggle. This stems from the recovering people-pleasing side of me that doesn't want to put anyone out. My ego dislikes admitting I can't do something by myself because sometimes that feels like I am not smart or good enough for the challenge.

Learning to embrace the help and support of others has been extremely rewarding for me. This hasn't necessarily been giant gestures—it's the little things like asking someone to give me feedback on a project. Or asking my partner to pick up some of my parenting slack because I need dedicated time to work solo.

Driven people can take on a lot—sometimes to our own detriment. We often feel the need to care for everyone around us. That's awesome, but we must allow loved ones to take care of us occasionally, too.

Not only will accepting help aid the overall quality of our craft, it will help us not turn into walking nightmares trying to do all the things. Smart people ask questions, and strong people seek help.

Compliments Are an Act of Love—Don't Be a Dick

Until I was about college age, I had a very difficult time receiving compliments, honestly, because growing up, I didn't get many—especially about the way I looked. When people would compliment me, I would feel embarrassed and make a self-deprecating joke.

Once after one of these awkward encounters, a woman complimenting me could see my discomfort in being praised. With empathy, she explained to me that she, too, used to have trouble accepting admiration of any kind. Then one day she heard that when someone compliments you, it is their way of giving you a gift. When we reject their compliment or act as if we don't want it, it's the same as turning our nose up at a thoughtful gift our friend is trying to give us.

After this lightbulb moment, I began simply saying "thank you" when someone would compliment me. Just that was difficult to do for years. It was really hard at first to not reply with sarcasm or self-deprecation, but with practice, it got easier. Ten years later, I have no trouble accepting compliments—unless they're backhanded, of course. Ain't nobody got time for that.

A FEW SIMPLE WAYS WE CAN ACCEPT LOVE FROM OTHERS

- When someone offers their help, accept it and give up some control.
- Say "thank you" to compliments and gestures of love.
- Ask for feedback or advice. Listen.
- If someone asks you if you need anything, be honest.
- Ask for more time on a project or to reschedule a social event when you're overwhelmed.

Love Your Success

The same way I struggled to accept compliments, I'm now learning to never apologize for my success. I'm usually able to celebrate myself better in writing or on social media, but in person I've avoided talking about my work with people. I was attending a friend's wedding this past summer (congrats again, Julia!), and a wonderful mutual friend, Rachelle, was telling people at cocktail hour about how well my podcast was doing. I didn't know why, but I felt so embarrassed and even felt my rosacea flare up for a second, I swear.

She noticed my discomfort, and when we were alone, she said, "Tiffany! Why aren't you, like, celebrating your hard work? You're so quiet and reserved about it!" This was another unlock for me. I realized I did this as a way to (again) deflect the compliment or make other people comfortable. I didn't want to make anyone feel bad or like I was some uppity bitch. The thing is, I'm not an uppity bitch, so I need to trust that people who really know me and love me want to encourage my achievements as much as I want to honor theirs.

Over time and with practice, I have gotten a bit better. Before this aha moment, when someone would say something nice about my success, I would say something like, "What the fuck, right? No idea how that happened!" Spoiler alert: I know exactly how it happened. Through countless hours of hard work. It has been so ingrained in me to make myself small that I never learned how to be proud of myself.

I committed to breaking this habit the same way I began accepting compliments as gifts. Now when someone tells me that they appreciate my art, I focus on thanking them for their support and say things like "Thank you, I'm really proud of myself" or "Thanks, I've really enjoyed working on that."

My success doesn't take away from anyone else's; therefore, I have no reason to diminish my achievements or discredit myself—and neither should you.

Love the Journey (for Real, Though)

Implementing the things you've learned in this book will take self-compassion, resilience, and perseverance. Progress isn't always linear, and it's important to recognize that great things take time. We are human; we will make mistakes, forget things, say the wrong things, and royally fuck up at times. Do not let perceived failures keep you from real progress.

Look at your action plan as an adventure. Just because it's challenging doesn't mean it isn't also fun! In fact, if you're not enjoying the journey, consider whether you're truly pursuing your passions. It's okay to change your mind and pivot—just keep moving.

I've worked my ass off (thankfully not actually off) and enjoyed the hell out of it! There have been so many challenges over the past few years while pursuing my goals, and there will be many more that I will have to continually crush in the future. It's all been worth it. It's changed my life and the lives of others. When we allow ourselves to shine, we help others do the same.

Love Your Determination

First of all, the fact that you've made it to this point in the book tells me you are awesome AF and ready to take the next step toward your highest self! You've already invested in your personal growth, and that is something to celebrate.

As you go forth and prosper, remember to honor your progress and internalize your successes. I personally like to plan little rewards for myself as a way to motivate and recognize my work. Sometimes this is something as simple as a quiet bath after a long day of editing. Don't wait for someone else to celebrate you; be your own cheering section. And yell loudly AF.

CLOSING TIME

Back in chapter 1, I asked you, "What ingredients do you think make a strong person?" Now that you have finished this book, have there been any changes to your formula?

_____

_____

_____

_____

_____

What are a few things this book has helped you realize about yourself?

_____

_____

_____

_____

_____

_____

What are you most excited to get started on moving forward?

_____

_____

_____

_____

_____

What are five things you are proud of yourself for already? (Hint: Finishing this book counts as one of them!)

_____

_____

_____

_____

_____

_____

HUMBLE
Thy
ASS.

Glossary

abundance – Having more than enough of a feeling, object, wealth, or attitude

abundance mentality – The ideology that there is enough success, love, and opportunities to go around for everyone

action plan – A detailed outline of the actions needed to reach a goal

anxiety – 1. A feeling of uneasiness in our minds 2. Out-of-control, fear-driven doubt and negativity that distracts us

balance – Equality or equivalence in weight, parts, schedule, or emotion

body image – The way we view our own body and how we feel about it

change – The feeling or description of something new, fresh, and/or developing. Smething different than its original form

cheap talk – Communication between players (often in video games) that does not directly affect the payoffs of the game. Conversation (usually shallow) that doesn't concern the real subject or purpose of the conversation

commit – Promise to execute an action

confidence – Full trust in ourselves or in others' abilities. Accepting our imperfect human nature and loving ourselves regardless

conscious – The stuff we're thinking about right now. The part of our brain we use in the moment—with our homies the five senses

depression – A sometimes soul-sucking empty feeling of emotional dead inside-ness. Prolonged feelings of sadness that make you want to withdraw from life, isolate yourself to your bed, and watch mindless TV while you shovel cookie dough into your mouth

discomfort – A lack of comfort. For example, the way I feel when I have to take a dump in a public restroom

ego – Our individual self-esteem or self-importance. The level at which we view our importance

egotistical – Conceited, pretentious, self-centered, annoying AF

energy – 1. The emotional output or vibes humans or environments give off 2. The amount of give-a-fuck required for completing mental, emotional, or physical tasks

failure – An outcome we regard as unsuccessful, lacking purpose or growth

faith – Unconditional belief in and trust in something or someone

fake it 'til you make it – An English saying that implies if we imitate competence, confidence, and an optimistic growth mindset, we can accomplish our desired results with time, experience, and practice

fear – The (real or imagined) distressing emotion of dread, impending danger, compromised safety, looming threats of pain, injury, or death

fixed mindset – Being shortsighted AF. Being a rigid little bitch. Believing that our capabilities are fixed traits and that "natural talent" or past events dictate our future outcomes

forgive – 1. To stop resenting someone or something
2. To make peace with hard shit in order to free ourselves

generous – The act or idea of being giving, charitable, considerate, big-hearted, hospitable, unselfish

gratitude – The art of being thankful for all that you already have in life. Celebrating the ways in which we are blessed and showing true appreciation

growth mindset – The belief that everyone's abilities can be developed through commitment and hard-ass work

habit – A pattern of choice we make consciously and subconsciously in our lives

hater – A person who greatly dislikes a specified person or thing. A negative or critical person that is probs just projecting their insecurity or scarcity/fixed mindset on others

Internet troll – Bored AF dicks who pick fights online or say wild shit to get the attention or approval of other people online. Cowards who harass, criticize, bully, antagonize, or lie about others as a way to distract themselves from their self-hatred

meditate – Focusing our attention inward, thinking deeply

mental health – 1. Our psychological wellness, health, strength. The quality in which we navigate life and all its fuckery 2. The area of psychology that studies how TF we are handling life

mindfulness – Being present in our current moment in time. Focusing our attention on what's happening IRL

mindset – The attitude with which we think about ourselves, others, and the situations around us

money mindset – 1. The attitude with which you think about your finances and financial capabilities 2. The influence you have in making key financial decisions

narcissism – 1. The belief that one's needs, feelings, ideas, or beliefs are more important than those of others. Selfishness 2. Excessive infatuation with oneself

passion – The stuff that makes us want to get out of bed on a rainy Sunday. A deep enthusiasm or love for something

perfectionism – Our egotistical hustle to try to convince others and ourselves we are worthy of love and acceptance. An unattainable goal

prioritize – Determine what is most timely and important

procrastination – 1. Avoiding important shit with very unimportant shit 2. Putting off starting a project or event that's important to us, usually because we are afraid of being imperfect

purpose – 1. The reason for which we exist 2. The motivation to reach a desired result 3. Grit, determination, resoluteness, tenacity

reality – The state or quality of being real, hashtag authentic. Facts. Receipts. Real shit

resentment – The displeasure, sadness, or rage we feel toward an act, remark, or person who we feel has injured or harmed us

rut – Feeling stale, bored, unsettled, uninspired, or rigid

scarcity – Short or dwindling supply of something. Insufficiency or infrequency

scarcity mindset – The belief that someone else having something will keep others from having it

self-care – The care of ourselves without the assistance of others. Prioritization of our needs

self-compassion – 1. Forgiveness or empathy toward ourselves 2. Accepting our imperfections with love

self-image – The way we see ourselves. The ideas we have about who we are

self-love – The love we have for ourselves

self-perception – How you see yourself and your individual impact. Self-awareness

self-talk – The language and manner we use to talk to ourselves

shame – The humiliation and/or anxiety and/or sadness that comes from the feeling of being wrong, foolish, imperfect, etc.

sign – 1. Any person, place, thing, action, event, or pattern we interpret to have meaning other than what is originally intended 2. An indication, clue, or token from our life that we feel conveys a meaning

soulmate – A being that is flawlessly suited to be in a relationship with another

subconscious – Our brain's hard drive. The place we store all of our memories and shit

success – 1. The desired outcome of attempted endeavors 2. Accomplishing our intended goals

values – Our core beliefs that comprise who we are and what is important to us. Things we believe deeply in and consider important in life

vibration – Our emotional tone, impact, atmosphere, state of being. The energy we give off to others around us

vulnerability – The act of being open and exposing your authentic self and beliefs to others, despite the possibility that others may judge or harm you

wealth – 1. A surplus of money or valuable shit
2. An abundance of anything

COCK 🍆
BLOCK
DOUBT
and EXCUSES

Resources

The National Domestic Violence Hotline
1-800-799-SAFE (7233) or 1-800-787-3224 (TTY)
www.adwas.org
Video phone (only for deaf callers): 1-855-812-1001
Email: nationaldeafhotline@adwas.org

National Suicide Prevention Lifeline
1-800-273-8255
The National Suicide Prevention Lifeline is free and confidential, and is intended as a lifeline for those in crisis or distress as well as those hoping to prevent a crisis. It is also an excellent resource for those whose loved ones are having or are at risk of experiencing a mental health crisis.

Psychology Today
www.psychologytoday.com
A free listing of licensed therapists.

The Body Positive
www.thebodypositive.org
A nonprofit organization working to "end the harmful consequences of negative body image," which include but aren't limited to self harm, eating disorders, being at higher risk for experiencing abusive relationships, addiction, and suicidal crisis.

References

Brockway, Laurie Sue. "11 Inspiring Quotes about Self-Love." *Huffington Post*. May 24, 2014.

Cherry, Kendra. "The Role of the Conscious Mind." *Very Well Mind*. September 29, 2019.

Chopra, D. "6 Steps for Creating Spiritual Abundance." *The Chopra Center*, Chopra.com. https://chopra.com/articles/6-steps-for-creating-abundance

Covey, Stephen. *The 7 Habits of Highly Effective People*. Free Press, 1989.

Economy, Peter. "17 Growth Mindset Quotes That Will Inspire Your Success and Happiness." *Inc.* September 6, 2018.

Economy, Peter. "26 Brilliant Quotes on the Super Power of Words." *Inc.* November 5, 2015.

Elkeles, Simone. *How to Ruin a Summer Vacation*. Woodbury, MN: Flux, 2006.

Harvard Women's Health Watch. "The Health Benefits of Strong Relationships." August 6, 2019.

Heisler, Melissa. "Why Stay Angry?" *Huffington Post*. April 6, 2016.

Holmes, Lindsay. "6 Times Michelle Obama Stood Up for Mental Health." *Huffington Post*. November 14, 2016.

Jacobs, Leanne. *Beautiful Money*. New York: Penguin Random House, 2017.

Kerpen, Dave. "15 Inspiring Quotes on Passion (Get Back to What You Love)." *Inc.* March 27, 2014.

Kross, Ethan. "Self-Talk as a Regulatory Mechanism: How You Do It Matters." *Journal of Personality and Social Psychology* 106, no. 2 (2014): 304–24. doi:10.1037/a0035173.

Leadem, Rose. "12 Leaders, Entrepreneurs and Celebrities Who Have Struggled with Imposter Syndrome," *Entrepreneur*. November 8, 2017.

Lorde, Audre. *A Burst of Light: And Other Essays*. Firebrand Books, 1988.

Mayo Clinic. "Depression (Major Depressive Disorder)." Accessed December 18, 2019.

McKelle, Erin. "20 Body Image Quotes for Your Next Bad Day, Because Your Body Isn't the Problem." *Bustle*. June 15, 2015.

Medrut, Flavia. "25 Brené Brown Quotes on Courage, Vulnerability, and Shame." *Goalcast*. June 19, 2019.

Morin, Amy. "7 Scientifically Proven Benefits of Gratitude." *Psychology Today*. April 3, 2015.

O'Keefe, Paul A., Carol S. Dweck, and Gregory M. Walton. "Implicit Theories of Interest: Finding Your Passion or Developing It?" *Psychological Science* 29, no. 10 (September 2018): 1653-64. doi:10.1177/0956797618780643.

Pinker, Susan. "The Secret to Living Longer May Be Your Social Life." Filmed April 2017 in Toronto, Canada. TED video, 15:55. https://www.ted.com/talks/susan_pinker_the_secret_to_living_longer_may_be_your_social_life.

Positive Psychology Institute. "What Is Positive Psychology?" Accessed December 18, 2019.

Random House Unabridged Dictionary of American English, Random House, 2019.

Riggan, William. *Picaros, Madmen, Naifs, and Clowns: The Unreliable First-Person Narrator*. University of Oklahoma Press, 1982.

Sakulku, Jaruwan, and James Alexander. "The Impostor Phenomenon." *International Journal of Behavioral Science* 6, no. 1 (2011): 73-92.

Seligman, Martin E. P., and Mihaly Csikszentmihalyi. "Positive Psychology: An Introduction." *American Psychologist* 55, no. 1 (2000): 5–14. doi:10.1037/0003-066X.55.1.5.

Shinn, Florence Scovel. *The Complete Works of Florence Scovel Shinn*. Mineola, NY: Dover Publications, 2010.

Steele, Claude M. "The Psychology of Self-Affirmation: Sustaining the Integrity of the Self." *Advances in Experimental Social Psychology* 21 (1988): 261–302.

Sweatt, Lydia. "19 Motivational Quotes to Help You Get Sh*t Done." *Success*. March 2, 2017.

Taibbi, Robert. "How to Break Bad Habits." *Psychology Today*. December 15, 2017.

Weir, Kirsten. "Feel Like a Fraud?" *GradPSYCH Magazine* 11, no. 4 (November 2013): 24.

Index

Acknowledgments

THANK YOU to all who have helped me transform my pain into passion: Michael, Jude, Ruby, Ozzy, Bobby, Ari, Alfie, Rufus, Papa, Lita, Nicole, Danny, MeMa Hope, Kelly Kae, Elaine Fischer, Sara Lewis, Alissa Doyle, Isaac Smith, Morgan Shanahan, Jill Krause, Darah Shawn, Lauren Jenkins, Julia Valdez, Amanda Rose Photography, AF's, JBR, the Reeses, the Negrons, the Smiths, the Greeleys, the Allens, the Doyles, the Gordons, the Lewises, the Jetts, the Gollings, the Bellamys, the Klimas, the Barstows, podcast listeners, book readers, Mom2Summit, BuzzFeed, Audioboom, Stitch fam, Zoloft, feminism, 49ers, Togo's roast beef and cheddar sandwiches on classic white with no lettuce, dry shampoo, caffeine, THC, Dutch Bros, my eyebrows, therapy, Google Calendar, See's Candies, music, sugar, *Seinfeld*, expletives, and haters.

About the Author

Tiffany Reese is a writer, podcaster, and body-positive stylist based in northern California. Tiffany began blogging professionally in 2012 at LookieBoo.com, a children's fashion and lifestyle site. In 2019, Tiffany created the Iris Award–winning, top-performing podcast *Something Was Wrong*, which aims to validate victims of emotional abuse, coercive control, and gaslighting, and educate the public in the process. She also released her first book, *Everything Sucks: A Gratitude Journal for People Who Have Been Through Some Sh*t.*